FAVORITE RECIPES

35 YEARS OF KANSAS PRIZEWINNERS FROM THE WICHITA EAGLE

COMPILED BY

KATHLEEN KELLY

Dedicated to joyful eaters and enthusiastic cooks of the past, present and future

And especially to Lauren Geneva Humphries

Printed in the United States of America by Mennonite Press, Inc., Newton, Kan.

ISBN 1-880652-20-X
Library of Congress Catalog Number 93-60405

Cover photography by Mike Hutmacher
Cover design and interior art by Sara Quinn
Book design by John Hiebert
Edited by Chuck Potter

Contents

Introduction

Homo sapiens have been sharing recipes since fire was discovered and the first caveman or cavewoman accidentally dropped a hunk of meat into the flames and hurried to tell other members of the clan how good it tasted.

Today, cookbook collections, card files and shoe boxes full of clippings are both a delight and a despair in every kitchen.

Recipes used most often once were likely to be those handed down from generation to generation in a family, or acquired from friends. Today we have added recipes from food product labels, appliance manufacturers and television cooking shows. This tradition of sharing favorite recipes was the impetus for The Wichita Eagle's recipe contest, which began in 1955 under the guidance of Ruth Meyer. Now retired from The Eagle for many years, Ruth lives in Marion.

I became The Eagle's home economist in 1955, but didn't work with the recipe contest until 1957.

Entries in the early Favorite Recipe contests were judged by panels of home economists, usually on paper without testing the recipes. In 1958 we worked with a foods class in the home economics department at Wichita State University (one of the last before the department was disbanded) to judge the contest.The students screened the recipes, tested those they thought had merit and let taste appeal be their final guide to selecting winners.

Today, recipe screening and test cooking are done by Eagle staff members. Home economists, dietitians and just-plain-cooks evaluate the recipes for ease of preparation, appearance of the final product and cost. Eagle employees and visitors rate, taste and comment on the finished products. All of these factors are considered when prizes are awarded.

Through the years the contest and cookbook have had a variety of rules, classifications, titles and months of publication. Prizes have ranged from merchandise such as a microwave oven to silver dollars mounted in plaques and engraved silver spoons. In recent years Kansas-made items such as baskets, pottery and food have been rewards for the winning cooks.

In the early years many women cooks used their married titles — Mrs. John Doe — but given names are used today. In this book you'll find recipe attribution in both forms. Home cooking was still "women's work" and for several years there was a "For Men Only" classification to encourage them to enter. There also have been special classifications for young people.

Ingredients have changed, too. One had to hunt for commercial sour cream in Kansas in 1955, and yogurt was equally rare in the dairy products refrigerator. No one had ever heard of lemon pepper or the many other spice and seasoning blends available today. Mixes and convenience foods were just beginning to be a factor in the marketplace.

And weight of contents in cans has changed. If the can of tomatoes or corn available for use in a recipe calling for 16 ounces contains only 15½ ounces, go ahead and use it.

The recipes in this collection are only some of those that have won prizes and an even lower percentage of the thousands and thousands of contest recipes that have been published in Eagle cookbooks since 1955.

They have been selected to give a well-rounded collection of recipes with which to plan parties and family meals. Don't expect to find basic recipes for biscuits and chocolate cake. Originality is considered when the Favorite Recipe Contest is judged, so the recipes showcase the creativity of the cooks who submitted them.

All the cooks who have submitted recipes in any of The Eagle's Favorite Recipe contests make this collection possible, whether or not their names appear. We at The Eagle hope you will continue to share your recipes for years to come.

Kathleen Kelly
Home Economist
The Wichita Eagle
March 1993

APPETIZERS AND CONDIMENTS

Hospitable Kansans always have plenty of entertaining ideas for the Favorite Recipe Contest. The recipes become more substantial each year, probably because changing lifestyles have many Americans snacking and grazing their way through the day.

Trays of tiny cucumber sandwiches have been replaced by savory cheese dips and baked or microwaved tidbits served piping hot.

In Kansas, potato and corn chips have taken a backseat to more substantial tortilla chips.

Recipes submitted in recent years reflect the increased informality of entertaining. Readers seem to be telling us that good food and good company make good parties, not expensive foods in lavish settings.

In this chapter you'll also find prizewinning recipes for beverages and condiments. Many of the condiments were submitted as recipes for canning and freezing. Today more cooks put foods by for special occasions and gifts than fill the cellar with canned tomatoes and peaches.

APPETIZERS

Sausage and Apple Appetizers

- **2 tablespoons butter or margarine**
- **1 large onion, chopped**
- **½ cup apple jelly**
- **½ cup firmly packed brown sugar**
- **2 lbs. cocktail-size smoked sausages**
- **3 apples, peeled, cored and sliced**
- **1 tablespoon cornstarch**
- **2 tablespoons warm water**

In a large skillet melt butter over medium-high heat. Add onion and saute, stirring constantly, until onion is golden. Stir in apple jelly and brown sugar. Add sausages and reduce heat to medium-low. Cook, stirring occasionally, 20 minutes or until mixture begins to thicken. Add apples, partially cover pan, and cook 10 minutes or until apples are tender. Combine cornstarch and water and stir into mixture in pan. Cook 2 to 3 minutes more or until mixture thickens. Serve warm. Makes 30 appetizers.

Jacqueline Crossman, Hutchinson, 1990

Satan Wings and Sauce

2 lbs. chicken wings
1 teaspoon salt
½ teaspoon red pepper
½ cup flour
¼ teaspoon black pepper

Satan Sauce

1 tablespoon red pepper flakes
2 tablespoons lemon juice
2 tablespoons hot sauce
2 tablespoons vinegar
⅛ teaspoon salt
¼ cup ketchup
½ cup melted butter

Split chicken wings at joints; discard tips. Combine salt, red pepper, flour and black pepper in plastic bag; shake and mix. Place 3 or 4 pieces of chicken in bag; shake well to coat. Repeat procedure with remaining chicken. Heat 1 inch of oil in a large skillet to 325 degrees. Add chicken and fry 20 minutes until golden brown on both sides. Drain on paper towels and serve with sauce. For sauce, place red pepper flakes in blender; blend 30 seconds. Add lemon juice, hot sauce, vinegar, salt and ketchup. Blend 30 seconds. Blend on low speed while adding butter in slow, steady stream. Blend on high until thick. Makes 1 cup.

Mary Jo White, Summerfield, 1990

Ultimate Chili Dip

2 lbs. ground round
1 cup chopped onion
2 cloves garlic, minced
1 pkg. (2 lbs.) processed American cheese, cut in pieces
1 can (16 oz.) chili beans, with liquid
¾ cup evaporated milk
2 pkgs. (1 ¾ oz. each) chili seasoning mix
½ cup chopped jalapenos
  Tortilla and corn chips (16 oz. bag) to serve

In large Dutch oven cook meat, onion and garlic over medium heat until meat is brown; drain. Add cheese, beans, evaporated milk, chili seasoning and jalapenos to meat mixture; stir. Cook over medium heat, stirring often, until thoroughly blended and heated through. Serve warm in a chafing dish with tortilla or corn chips. Makes 10 cups dip.

Verdel Krug, La Crosse, 1988

Aloha Dip

12 coconut macaroons, crushed in small pieces
¼ cup firmly packed light brown sugar
1 pint (16 oz.) dairy sour cream
1 large pineapple
  Assorted berries, seedless green grapes, sliced peaches or other fresh fruits

In small bowl mix macaroons, sugar and sour cream. Chill several hours to soften macaroons. Do not stir again or macaroon crumbs will break into small pieces. Slice a cap-shaped piece off pineapple top, about 1 inch below leaves. Hollow out center of pineapple. Leave a firm shell to hold dip. Cut fruit in small pieces, discarding core. Fill shell with dip. Replace top, if desired. Place in center of large platter. Arrange pineapple chunks, assorted berries, grapes and peaches in groups around the pineapple. Makes 1 quart dip.

Paula G. Webb, Wichita, 1987

Bombay Vegetable Dip

1 cup mayonnaise
1 teaspoon prepared horseradish
1 teaspoon curry powder
1 teaspoon vinegar
2 tablespoons dried onion
1 teaspoon garlic salt
Raw vegetables for dipping

In small bowl combine mayonnaise, horseradish, curry, vinegar, onion and garlic salt. Mix well. Best if refrigerated 2 hours or more. Serve with raw vegetables.

Chris Hutchens, Wellington, 1986

Layered Shrimp Dip

8 oz. cream cheese, softened
6 oz. thick chili sauce
4 to 5 sliced green onions
¼ cup green pepper, diced
1 can (4 ¼ oz.) sliced black olives
1 can (4 ¼ oz.) small shrimp, drained
1 cup shredded mozzarella cheese
Party crackers or chips

In pizza plate or platter, start with softened cheese and layer chili sauce, onions, green pepper, olives, shrimp and cheese in order listed. Refrigerate until serving time. Serve with crackers or chips. Makes 10 servings.

Leigh Ann Kloefkorn, Wichita, 1986

Josefinas

2 sticks (4 oz. each) butter
1 cup mayonnaise
2 cans (4 oz. each) diced green chilies, undrained
1 clove garlic, peeled, sliced thin or mashed
  Thinly sliced French bread or crackers
1 lb. Monterey Jack cheese, grated
  Paprika

In small bowl soften butter and blend with mayonnaise, chilies and garlic. Spread on thinly sliced French bread or crackers of your choice. Top each with cheese and sprinkle with paprika; toast under broiler until mix is melted and slightly browned. Makes about 3 cups spread.

This is a very good — but fattening — spread. Can be kept in refrigerator indefinitely.

Rosemary Wilkerson, Dodge City, 1986

Crostini

12 slices firm white bread
5 tablespoons butter, divided
2 tablespoons all-purpose flour
½ cup milk
3 oz. fresh mushrooms (about 9 medium), finely chopped
6 tablespoons grated Parmesan cheese
2 teaspoons anchovy paste
¼ teaspoon salt
⅛ teaspoon pepper
Green and ripe olive halves (optional)
Red and green bell pepper strips (optional)
Anchovy fillets (optional)

Heat oven to 350 degrees. Cut circles out of bread slices with 2-inch round cutter. Melt 3 tablespoons butter in small saucepan. Brush both sides of bread circles lightly with butter. Bake bread circles on ungreased baking sheet, turning circles once, until golden brown, about 5 to 6 minutes per side. Melt remaining 2 tablespoons butter in small saucepan. Stir in flour; cook and stir over medium heat until bubbly. Whisk in milk; cook, stirring constantly, until sauce thickens and bubbles for 1 minute. Sauce will be very thick. Stir sauce into chopped mushrooms. Mix in 3 tablespoons of the cheese and the anchovy paste, salt and pepper. Spread a heaping teaspoon of mushroom mixture on top of each toast round. Place on ungreased baking sheet and sprinkle with remaining 3 tablespoons cheese. Decorate with olive halves, pepper strips or anchovy fillets. Bake at 425 degrees until tops are lightly browned, 5 to 7 minutes. Serve hot. Makes 2 dozen crostini.

Note: Thin slices of small-diameter baguette loaf may be substituted for sliced bread rounds.

Jan Hillard, Wichita, 1985

Almost-Boursin Cheese Appetizers

2 cloves garlic
8 oz. cream cheese, softened
1 tablespoon butter, softened
1 teaspoon parsley
⅛ teaspoon marjoram
⅛ teaspoon thyme
⅛ teaspoon basil
¾ teaspoon red wine vinegar
½ teaspoon Worcestershire sauce
Minced parsley (optional)

Place garlic cloves in food processor and mince finely. Add cream cheese, butter, parsley, marjoram, thyme, basil, vinegar and Worcestershire. Process until well mixed. Mixture may be packed in a crock or serving dish, or formed into a ball and rolled in minced parsley. Refrigerate several hours or overnight until firm. Serve with crackers. Makes about 1¼ cups.

Sandra Piech-Lentini, Wichita, 1984

Confetti Dip

1 pkg. (8 oz.) cream cheese, softened
3 green onions, finely sliced (include tops)
1 can (10 ¾ oz.) cream of mushroom soup
1 pkg. (about 4 oz.) dried beef, shredded
1 teaspoon Worcestershire sauce
Crackers, potato chips or corn chips

In small bowl stir cheese with a spoon until creamy. Stir in onions, mushroom soup, dried beef and Worcestershire. Mix until thoroughly blended. Chill. Serve with crackers, potato chips or corn chips. Makes about 2 cups dip.

Mrs. Frederick Suderman, Wichita, 1965

Curry Dip Superb

1 cup mayonnaise
⅔ teaspoon dry mustard
1 ½ teaspoons curry powder
⅛ teaspoon salt
⅔ tablespoon lemon juice
Vegetables for dipping

In small bowl blend mayonnaise, mustard, curry, salt and lemon juice. Chill to blend flavors. Use as dip for fresh celery, carrot sticks, green onions, radishes or cauliflower florets. May be used as sauce for fish and shrimp. Makes about 1 cup.

Mrs. Percy Wendt, Herington, 1973

Shrimp Dip

1 envelope plain gelatin
¼ cup hot water
1 can (10 ¾ oz.) tomato soup
1 pkg. (8 oz.) cream cheese
1 cup mayonnaise
1 cup chopped celery
1 medium onion, chopped
3 hard-cooked eggs, chopped
2 cans (6 ½ oz. each) medium shrimp, drained
Potato chips or corn chips

In cup or small bowl dissolve gelatin in hot water and set aside to cool. Mix tomato soup and cream cheese in double boiler and melt over boiling water. Stir with wire whisk. Remove from heat and add cooled gelatin mixture. Fold in mayonnaise and whisk until smooth. Add celery, onion, eggs and shrimp. Chill several hours. Serve with chips or corn snacks. Makes about 1½ quarts.

Aileen Cook, Medicine Lodge, 1978

Italian Cracker Spread

1 **medium-large eggplant (about 1 ½ lbs.)**
1 **large tomato**
½ **cup finely chopped onion**
1 **clove garlic, minced**
1 **teaspoon sugar**
¼ **cup olive or salad oil**
2 **tablespoons lemon juice**
2 **teaspoons minced parsley**
  Crackers or party rye slices

Preheat oven to 375 degrees. Pierce whole unpeeled eggplant with fork in several places and place in a shallow greased baking pan. Bake 30 minutes in preheated oven, or until soft. Let cool; peel and finely dice pulp into medium bowl. Drop tomato in a small pan of boiling water for a few seconds, run tomato under cold water, peel and finely chop. Mix diced eggplant, chopped tomato, onion, garlic, sugar, oil, lemon juice and parsley. Chill thoroughly. Serve with crackers or party rye slices. Makes 12 appetizer or snack servings.

Joan Barrier, Wichita, 1975

Baby Drumsticks

  2 cups fine dry crumbs (pretzels or crackers)
  ¾ cup grated Parmesan cheese
  ¼ cup chopped parsley
  1 clove garlic, crushed
  2 teaspoons salt
  ⅛ teaspoon pepper (or more)
 20 (approximately) baby drumsticks (chicken wings with
      the two smaller appendages removed)
  ¼ lb. butter, melted

In shallow bowl combine crumbs, cheese, parsley, garlic, salt and pepper. Dip each baby drumstick into melted butter, then into crumb mixture, coating well. Place in baking dish; do not overlap. Pour on remaining butter. Bake in 350- to 375-degree oven 1 hour or until tender and crusty. Makes 20 drumsticks.

Note: If desired, discard only wing tip and prepare first and second joint pieces.

Mrs. Robert N. Barnhart, Salina, 1969

Bowknots

  1 loaf fresh sandwich bread, thinly sliced
  1 can (10 ¾ oz.) cream of mushroom soup
 24 bacon strips about 4 inches long
 24 wooden toothpicks

Trim all crust from bread. Spread soup on one side of bread slices, being careful to cover edges. Roll from corner to opposite corner. Wrap a bacon strip around the middle of each roll and secure with a wooden toothpick. Place on a cookie sheet and bake 1 hour in 200-degree oven. The bowknots will be dry, crisp and delicious. Makes about 2 dozen appetizers.

Note: Prepared rolls may be frozen before baking, wrapped and stored in freezer and baked a few at a time.

Mrs. Howard M. McKee, Neodesha, 1974

Asparagus Roll Canapes

20 slices thin white sandwich bread
3 oz. blue cheese
8 oz. cream cheese
1 egg
20 fresh, frozen or canned asparagus spears
¼ lb. melted butter

Trim crusts off bread and flatten slices with rolling pin (about 4 at a time). In small bowl mix cheeses and egg; spread on each bread slice. Roll 1 asparagus spear in each slice, pressing to keep roll together. Pour butter in flat dish; dredge each roll-up in the butter. Place on cookie sheet and cut in thirds. Freeze on cookie sheet, then store in plastic bag. As needed, remove from freezer and bake on cookie sheet in 400-degree oven 10 to 15 minutes. Makes about 60 appetizers.

Margaret Rembleske, Wichita, 1982

Helen's Artichoke Appetizers

4 well-beaten eggs
3 tablespoons instant onion
¼ cup dry bread crumbs
½ teaspoon salt
⅛ teaspoon pepper
⅛ teaspoon crushed oregano
2 or 3 drops liquid hot sauce
2 cups grated sharp cheddar cheese
2 cans or jars (6 oz. each) marinated artichoke hearts, drained and finely chopped

In mixing bowl combine eggs, onion, crumbs, salt, pepper, oregano and hot sauce. Stir in cheese and artichoke hearts. Mix well. Spread in greased 8x8-inch pan. Bake in 350-degree oven 30 minutes or until set. Cut in squares and store in freezer, if desired. Serve hot or cold. Makes 16 to 20 appetizers.

Ann Stephens, Garden City, 1982

Rum Tum Tiddy

1 can (10 ½ oz.) condensed tomato soup
½ lb. sharp cheese, cut in small pieces
½ cup salsa
Salt and pepper
Crackers and chips

In saucepan mix tomato soup and small pieces of cheese. Cook and stir over low heat or in double boiler until the cheese melts. Add salsa and heat approximately 5 minutes. Season to taste with salt and pepper. Serve with crackers and chips. Makes 5 servings.

My mom introduced me to this recipe because it was easy and very good. When my friends drop in and we are hungry, we don't bother my mom. We just make this dip recipe and eat it right away.

Edward Sitz, Wichita, 1986

BEVERAGES

Cranberry Tea

1 **pint cranberry juice**
1 **quart apple juice**
1 **can (6 oz.) frozen orange juice**
1 **can (6 oz.) frozen lemonade**
2 **cups sugar**
5 **drops clove oil**
10 **drops cinnamon oil**

In refrigerator container combine fruit juices, lemonade, sugar and oils for concentrated tea. Refrigerate. When ready to use, dilute with water to taste and serve hot. Makes about 2 quarts concentrate.

Leona Whipple, Eureka, 1965

Rhubarb Punch

¾ **lb. rhubarb**
1 **quart water**
½ **cup sugar**
¼ **cup lemon juice**
¼ **cup orange juice**
3 **cups cold water**

Wash rhubarb but do not peel. Cut into small pieces. In saucepan cover rhubarb with 1 quart water. Cook until tender; strain into non-aluminum container. Add sugar and stir until dissolved. Add lemon and orange juices. Allow to cool. Add cold water and serve over ice. Makes about 2 quarts.

Note: For a sparkling drink, substitute ginger ale for the water in this recipe.

Blanche Harvey, Fredonia, 1958

Pineapple Mallowade

24 marshmallows
1 cup water
2 cups unsweetened pineapple juice
¼ cup lemon juice
⅛ teaspoon salt
3 cups pale dry ginger ale
Ice
Mint leaves (for garnish)

Place marshmallows and water in the top of a double boiler. Heat over boiling water until marshmallows are melted. Stir occasionally. Blend in fruit juices and salt. Mix well. Chill in refrigerator. Add ginger ale just before serving. Pour into ice-filled glasses. Garnish with mint leaves, if desired. Makes 6 to 8 servings.

Mrs. Dwight Goodman, Wellington, 1956

Go-Go Cocktail

3 cups tomato juice
3 tablespoons vinegar
2 tablespoons sugar
¾ bay leaf
3 teaspoons minced onion
2 tablespoons lemon juice
¾ cup diced celery

In large saucepan combine tomato juice, vinegar, sugar, bay leaf, onion, lemon juice and celery. Heat to boiling and simmer 10 minutes. Refrigerate overnight. Strain. Serve in cocktail glasses. Makes 8 servings.

Mrs. Floyd McJunkin, Toronto, 1967

Fruit Punch

1 can (6 oz.) frozen orange juice
2 cans (6 oz. each) frozen limeade
1 can (6 oz.) frozen lemonade
1 can (46 oz.) pineapple juice
1 pint cranberry juice cocktail
2 to 4 cups cold water
   Ice cubes
2 quarts ginger ale, chilled
1 quart plain soda water, chilled
   Fruit ice ring
   Mint leaves

Empty frozen juices, pineapple juice, cranberry juice and cold water into a large container. Let stand until frozen juices are thawed. Stir well. Pour mixture into punch bowl. Add ice cubes. Just before serving, gently pour in ginger ale and soda water. Top with fruit ice ring and sprigs of mint. Makes 30 servings.

Fruit ice ring: Use any combination of lime, lemon or orange slices. Arrange in a pattern on the bottom of an 8-inch ring mold. Add water to cover fruit. Freeze. Complete filling mold and freeze. To unmold, loosen ring by dipping bottom of mold into warm water. Float on top of punch and garnish with mint leaves.

Mrs. Merle V. Pearce, Wichita, 1956

Party Punch

2 cups orange juice
2 cups apple juice
2 cups cranberry juice cocktail
2 cups light corn syrup
1 cup lemon or lime juice
1 large bottle sparkling water
1 bottle champagne (optional)
Few sprigs of mint
Orange and lemon slices
Block of ice or ice cubes

In punch bowl combine orange, apple and cranberry juices, corn syrup, lemon juice, sparkling water and champagne (if desired). Add mint, orange and lemon slices and ice. Makes 30 servings.

Maurita Stearns, Wichita, 1962

Hot Cider Punch

1 ½ cups firmly packed brown sugar
1 cup granulated sugar
2 sticks cinnamon
6 whole cloves
1 quart apple cider
2 cans grapefruit juice
4 cups orange juice
2 cups lemon juice
Orange slices (optional)

Combine brown sugar, granulated sugar, cinnamon, cloves and apple cider in a large non-aluminum kettle. Bring to a boil. Boil 5 minutes. Stir occasionally. Add grapefruit, orange and lemon juices. Reheat to boiling point. Remove spices. Pour into cups and garnish with orange slices. Makes 40 servings.

Mrs. Carl H. Smith, Mulvane, 1962

Hot Party Punch

9 cups cranberry juice
9 cups unsweetened pineapple juice
4 ½ cups water
1 cup brown sugar
4 sticks cinnamon
¼ teaspoon salt
4 ½ teaspoons whole cloves
Orange slices

In bottom of 12-cup percolator, combine cranberry juice, pineapple juice, water and brown sugar. In percolator basket, combine cinnamon, salt and whole cloves. Plug in coffeepot and let it perk until it stops. Serve each cup garnished with an orange slice. Makes approximately 42 servings.

Mrs. Carl A. Smith, Liberal, 1969

Hot Buttered Cranberry Punch

2 cans (16 oz. each) jellied cranberry sauce
½ cup firmly packed brown sugar
4 cups water
¼ teaspoon salt
½ teaspoon cinnamon
½ teaspoon allspice
¼ teaspoon nutmeg
¾ teaspoon cloves
1 quart pineapple juice
Butter
Cinnamon sticks

In bowl crush cranberry sauce. In non-aluminum kettle combine brown sugar, 1 cup water, salt and spices. Bring to a boil. Add 3 cups water and beat until smooth. Add crushed cranberry sauce and pineapple juice. Simmer 5 minutes. Keep hot over hot water. Ladle into mugs, dot with butter and serve with cinnamon sticks. Makes 2½ quarts.

Mrs. Paul M. Johnson, Arkansas City, 1971

Indian Punch

   1 quart water
   1 lb. sugar
   1 lemon rind, grated
   2 cups strong tea
   1 teaspoon vanilla
   1 teaspoon almond extract
   3 lemons, juiced
   1 pint ginger ale
     Ice
     Water

In large, non-aluminum saucepan boil water, sugar and grated lemon rind 5 minutes. Strain into large container. Add tea, vanilla, almond extract and lemon juice. Cool. When ready to serve, place in punch bowl or pitchers and add ginger ale and ice. Add water to taste. Makes 12 to 15 servings.

Mrs. J.L. Foncannon, Wichita, 1958

West Indies Coffee

   ¼ cup instant coffee
   ¼ cup brown sugar
     Dash of salt
   3 ½ cups milk

In heat-proof pitcher combine coffee, brown sugar and salt. In saucepan or microwave container bring milk just to boil. Pour over coffee mixture, stirring to dissolve. Serve in mugs. Makes 4 to 6 servings.

Mrs. Eldon Bonham, Wichita, 1962

Pink Slushy Punch

1 pkg. (3 oz.) wild strawberry gelatin
2 cups sugar
2 cups boiling water
46 oz. pineapple juice
2 liters chilled lemon-lime carbonated beverage

In large bowl or heat-proof pitcher mix gelatin, sugar, boiling water and pineapple juice. Freeze in plastic gallon jar with wide mouth or milk carton container. Remove from freezer 1 hour before serving. Place in punch bowl. Add 2 liters chilled carbonated beverage and mix. Will be slushy. Makes 32 to 36 servings.

Dianne McCully, Wichita, 1990

Hawaiian Lemonade

1 can (6 oz.) frozen lemonade concentrate
1 can (6 oz.) water
1 can (12 oz.) apricot nectar, chilled
2 cans (6 oz. each) unsweetened pineapple juice, chilled
1 can (12 oz.) ginger ale, chilled
  Fresh pineapple wedges, quartered lime slices and/or maraschino cherries

In a large bowl or pitcher combine lemonade concentrate and 1 can water. Add apricot nectar and pineapple juice. Slowly pour ginger ale down side of bowl or pitcher. Stir gently with an up-and-down motion to mix. Serve over ice with pineapple, lime and cherries skewered on toothpicks. Makes five 8-ounce servings.

Louella Schmitz, Spivey, 1989

Brandy Slush

9 cups water
2 cups sugar
1 can (12 oz.) frozen lemonade concentrate
1 can (12 oz.) frozen orange juice concentrate
2 cups apricot brandy
Lemon-lime soda

In saucepan combine water and sugar; bring to boil. Let cool. In bowl or pitcher mix lemonade concentrate, orange juice concentrate and brandy; add water mixture and freeze. To serve, fill glasses ¾ full of slush, then fill with the soda. Makes 25 to 30 servings.

Lori Wellbrock, Hays, 1988

CONDIMENTS

Microwave Apple Butter

  1 **quart unsweetened applesauce**
1 ½ **to 2 cups granulated sugar**
  2 **tablespoons lemon juice**
  2 **teaspoons cinnamon**
  1 **teaspoon ginger**
  ½ **teaspoon cloves**
  ½ **teaspoon nutmeg**
  ½ **teaspoon salt**

Place applesauce in 2-quart, microwave-safe container; cover with food wrap; poke many holes to ventilate. Microwave on high 6 to 8 minutes until boiling. Mix sugar, lemon juice, cinnamon, ginger, cloves, nutmeg and salt into hot applesauce. Cover with ventilated wrap. Cook on high 15 minutes, stirring every 5 minutes. Carefully avoid steam to prevent burns. Pour into quart jar and keep refrigerated.

I put chunks of apples with peels from windfall apples in the freezer during summer and fall. I then cook a batch of apples and run them through a blender using a quart of sauce for apple butter. So easy and no scorching. You can have fresh apple butter even with purchased applesauce.

Maxine Mai, Lenora, 1990

Conserves

1 cup dried apricots
2 cups water
2 ¼ cups unsweetened pineapple tidbits
⅛ teaspoon salt
2 tablespoons lemon juice
1 cup sugar, or artificial sweetener to equal 1 cup sugar
½ cup nuts, finely chopped

In large saucepan simmer apricots in water until tender. Puree in blender or food processor. Drain pineapple tidbits; cut or dice into smaller pieces. Put apricot puree into saucepan; add pineapple, salt and lemon juice. Simmer, stirring constantly, about 5 minutes. Remove from heat; stir in sugar and nuts until sugar is dissolved. Fill 1-cup jelly jars, seal and process in hot water bath 20 minutes. Makes 2 cups.

Was my grandmother's, updated a little.

Lola Parker, Argonia, 1990

Green Relish Anytime of the Year

1 medium-large onion
1 medium dill pickle
1 large tart apple
2 heaping tablespoons sugar
1 cup cider vinegar

By hand or in food processor chop onion and dill pickle very fine. Do not grind. Add apple and chop again until fine. Turn into jar or refrigerator container with lid. Add sugar, stir well and add vinegar until it covers top of pickle mixture. Cover and store in refrigerator. This relish is splendid on meats, especially hamburgers. Makes 1 pint.

Frances Oliver, Derby, 1975

End of the Garden Relish

1 cup chopped cucumbers
1 cup chopped cabbage
1 cup chopped green peppers
1 cup thinly sliced onions
1 cup chopped green tomatoes
Salt water (½ cup salt for 2 quarts water)
1 cup chopped carrots
1 cup cauliflower pieces
1 cup green beans, cut in 1-inch pieces
1 cup chopped celery
1 tablespoon celery seed
2 tablespoons (or less) turmeric for color (optional)
2 cups vinegar
2 cups sugar

In large, non-aluminum container soak cucumbers, cabbage, peppers, onions and tomatoes in salt water overnight. Drain. In saucepans or microwave containers, cook carrots, cauliflower and green beans separately until tender. Mix all ingredients and boil 10 minutes. Pack into hot jars and while hot seal lids according to manufacturer's directions. Process in boiling water bath 10 minutes. Makes 3 pints.

Mrs. A.W. Rochs, Wichita, 1958

Horseradish Jelly

3 ¼ cups sugar
1 cup horseradish
½ cup cider vinegar
½ cup liquid fruit pectin

Combine sugar, horseradish and vinegar in large kettle. Bring to a boil and stir until sugar is dissolved. Add pectin and bring to rolling boil, stirring. Boil ½ minute. Skim; pour quickly into small gelatin molds. When firm, unmold and serve with beef pot roast. Makes 4 to 6 servings.

Mrs. L.A. Dunlap, Corbin, 1958

Olive Cherries

1 pint dark, sweet cherries
½ pint white vinegar
¼ pint cold water
1 tablespoon salt
2 tablespoons sugar

Wash cherries, leaving stems on. Put cherries into sterilized pint jar. In small bowl mix vinegar, water, salt and sugar. Pour over cherries. Seal jar lid according to manufacturer's directions. Repeat as desired. Process 10 minutes in boiling water bath. Ready to serve in about a week. Delicious with cold meats, ham and as a garnish.

Mrs. W.A. Palan, Arkansas City, 1957

Spiced Pickled Peaches

5 lbs. peaches
2 cups sugar
1 pint vinegar
2 cups light corn syrup
½ cup water
2 sticks (4 in. each) cinnamon
2 teaspoons whole cloves

Peel peaches by dipping in hot water to loosen skins. In large canning kettle boil sugar, vinegar, syrup, water, cinnamon and cloves 25 minutes. Place a few peaches in syrup and cook until tender. Remove with slotted spoon and place in sterilized jar. Repeat until all peaches are cooked. Place a few cloves and some of the cinnamon in each jar. Cover with syrup. Seal lids immediately according to manufacturer's directions. Process in boiling water bath 10 minutes. Makes 10 to 12 pints.
Note: Pears, nectarines or other fruit may be used.

Mrs. J.D. Vaughn, Wichita, 1960

Brandied Apricots

1 large can (28 oz.) whole apricots in light syrup
1 ½ cups brown sugar
½ cup brandy
½ stick cinnamon
12 whole cloves
1 tablespoon lemon juice
1 teaspoon grated lemon rind

Drain juice from apricots into saucepan. Add brown sugar, brandy and cinnamon stick. Boil 5 minutes. Skim off all foam. Stick 1 whole clove in stem end of each apricot. Add apricots, lemon juice and rind to syrup and simmer until thoroughly hot. Pack in sterilized glass jar and seal lid according to manufacturer's directions. Set aside to cool in a dark spot to ripen and develop that really brandied flavor. Makes 1 quart; serves 5 to 6.

Mamie Fly, Wichita, 1959

Pear Conserve

5 lbs. firm pears (15 cups, sliced)
10 cups sugar
1 lb. seedless raisins
Rind of 2 oranges
Juice of 3 oranges
Juice of 2 lemons

Peel pears and cut into small pieces. Place in large non-aluminum bowl or kettle. Add sugar and let stand overnight. Grind raisins and orange rind together; add with juices to pears. Cook until thick, about 1 hour and 20 minutes. Pour into sterilized jars and seal lids according to manufacturer's directions while hot. Process in boiling water bath 10 minutes. Makes about 6 pints.

Oleta Stabler, Wichita, 1970

Tomato Butter

7 lbs. tomatoes
3 ½ lbs. granulated sugar
1 tablespoon cinnamon
1 tablespoon mace
½ tablespoon cloves
1 tablespoon salt
1 pint vinegar

Peel tomatoes. In large canning kettle combine tomatoes, sugar, cinnamon, mace, cloves, salt and vinegar. Simmer until thick like jelly. Place in jars and seal according to manufacturer's directions. Process in boiling water bath for 10 minutes. Makes about 4 pints.

Eileen R. Entwisle, Wichita, 1956

Cajun Tiger Sauce

    4 large red tomatoes
    4 large green tomatoes
    2 large onions
    2 large green peppers
   12 jalapeno peppers
    2 cans (6 oz. each) tomato paste
    3 or 4 teaspoons garlic powder
  1 ½ cups vinegar
    2 tablespoons brown sugar

Run tomatoes, onions, green peppers and jalapenos through food grinder or chop finely in food processor. Place in large kettle and add tomato paste, garlic powder, vinegar and brown sugar; bring to a boil. If thicker sauce is preferred, boil to reduce to desired consistency. Remove from heat and pack in clean jars. Process in boiling water bath 30 minutes or in pressure canner 10 minutes at 5 lbs. pressure. Makes about 6 pints.

Note: This sauce can be used as a dip with corn chips, poured over cream cheese and "dipped" with corn chips, or used as a garnish on burritos, tacos, meat loaf, chicken-fried steak, omelets ... on and on.

Jan Preston, Newton, 1982

Freezer Corn

   18 cups fresh corn (cut from cobs)
    1 lb. butter or margarine
    1 pint half-and-half

Combine corn, butter and half-and-half in baking dish. Bake in 350-degree oven 1 hour, stirring occasionally. Cool and freeze in cartons.

Nila L. Denton, Stockton, 1985

Kiwi Jam

9 kiwifruit
6 cups granulated sugar
6 oz. liquid pectin
Green food coloring (optional)

Wash and sterilize canning jars, lids and bands. Peel and crush kiwifruit. In a large, heavy saucepan, combine crushed fruit and sugar. Stir well. Bring mixture to rolling boil, stirring constantly. Stir in liquid pectin. Return mixture to rolling boil, stirring constantly, and boil 1 minute. Remove from heat. Skim foam from top of mixture with a large metal spoon. If desired, stir in a few drops of food coloring to intensify color. Fill sterilized jars to within ¼ inch of tops. Wipe jar rims. Cover jars with lids and bands. Store in refrigerator or process in boiling water bath. Makes 6 cups jam.

I am very fond of kiwis, and this jam is a delightful change of pace.

Verdel Krug, La Crosse, 1989

Little Chicago Salsa

10 cups tomatoes, peeled, cored and chopped
1 ½ cups chopped onions
1 green pepper, chopped
2 cloves garlic, crushed or chopped
10 chili peppers (cayenne, jalapenos and tepins), more if you like it hotter
1 ½ cups white vinegar
1 ½ tablespoons cumin
2 tablespoons sugar
1 teaspoon salt
6 cups water
2 teaspoons dried oregano

In large canning kettle combine tomatoes, onions, green pepper, garlic, chili peppers, vinegar, cumin, sugar, salt, water and oregano. Bring to boil and simmer 30 minutes, stirring frequently. Cook longer for thicker salsa. Fill clean, hot pint jars. Leave ½-inch headspace. Process in boiling water bath 25 minutes. Makes 8 to 10 pints.

Rene Mares, Belleville, 1989

Wine Jelly

4 **cups wine (rose, white or red)**
6 **cups sugar**
1 **bottle (6 oz.) liquid fruit pectin**

In large kettle bring wine and sugar to rolling boil. Add pectin all at once. Cook 1 minute longer. Skim off froth. Pour in glasses and seal. Process in boiling water bath or refrigerate.
This is always in season and so easy.

Patsy Herrman, Garden Plain, 1988

Spiced Peach Jam

5 **cups fresh, unpeeled peaches (about 3 lbs.), crushed in blender**
¼ **cup lemon juice**
1 ½ **teaspoons cinnamon**
½ **teaspoon cloves**
¼ **teaspoon ginger**
1 **box (1 ¾ oz.) powdered pectin**
9 **cups (4 lbs.) sugar**

Place peaches in 6- or 8-quart saucepan. Add lemon juice, cinnamon, cloves, ginger and pectin. Place on heat and, stirring continuously to prevent scorching on the bottom, bring to full boil. Gradually add sugar, stirring to dissolve. Bring to full, rolling boil that cannot be stirred down, stirring constantly. Start timing and continue boiling 2 minutes. Remove pan from heat, and quickly skim with metal spoon to remove foam. Immediately fill hot, sterilized jars to about ¼ inch from the top and screw lids on tightly. Process in boiling water bath for 10 minutes. Let cool, undisturbed, for 24 hours. Makes 10 half-pint jars.

This comes from a cookbook I purchased at the famous Stephenson's Restaurants. They served it when we were there, and I thought it was so good.

Marlene Neufeld, Buhler, 1987

SOUPS

Kansans always have leaned toward hearty soups designed to be the main part of a meal, not a first course. Soup recipes submitted to the Favorite Recipe Contest have come from many heritages. They range from slow-cooked bean soups to quick concoctions put together with a can of this and a shake of that. When the Favorite Recipe Contest began, soup was considered family fare. It continues to solve problems for busy households where folks can't always sit down together for a meal. And there's never a problem with leftovers — soup often tastes even better the second time around. It even finds its way into the brown bag, to be reheated in the office microwave.

Today soup is a popular party food. A favorite way to entertain with soup is to invite guests for a kitchen party where everyone ladles from the pot, then cuts thick slices of warm bread.

Spaghetti-Corn Soup

1 envelope regular onion soup mix
2 cans (15 oz. each) spaghetti rings with meatballs in
  tomato sauce
1 can (16 oz.) cream-style corn
  Grated Parmesan cheese

In soup pot prepare onion soup mix according to package directions. Stir in spaghetti and meatballs and corn; heat thoroughly. Serve with grated Parmesan. Makes 8 servings.

Lester F. Guyer, Garden City, 1989

Ohio Tomato Bisque

2 thick or 4 thin slices bacon
1 can (20 oz.) stewed tomatoes
1 tablespoon red wine vinegar or Burgundy wine
1 tablespoon minced onion
½ teaspoon lemon pepper
½ to ¾ teaspoon Italian seasoning
¼ teaspoon dried basil
⅛ to ¼ teaspoon garlic salt or powder
1 can (10 ½ oz.) tomato soup
1 ½ cups half-and-half or milk

Cut bacon into ½-inch slices and fry in soup pot until crisp but not dry. Add cut-up tomatoes, vinegar or wine, onion, lemon pepper, Italian seasoning, basil and garlic. Simmer 5 minutes. Blend in undiluted tomato soup. Heat another 5 minutes; do not boil. Add half-and-half or milk and heat but do not boil or it will curdle. Makes 6 servings.

This is a recipe I'm often asked for after I've served it. Even if it does curdle it is still delicious and not unattractive.

Bettie Seibel, Peabody, 1990

Lantern House Hot and Sour Soup

4 cups chicken broth
½ teaspoon salt
4 tablespoons vinegar
1 teaspoon hot oil (see recipe)
1 tablespoon soy sauce
2 oz. canned baby shrimp
2 oz. bean curd (tofu), cubed
Few strips black mushroom
Few small diced pieces of bamboo shoots
Few small diced pieces of water chestnut
Chopped chives for garnish

In soup pot mix chicken broth, salt, vinegar, hot oil and soy sauce and bring to boil. Add shrimp, tofu, mushroom, bamboo shoots and water chestnut. Heat and serve at once with chives to garnish. Makes 4 servings.

Hot oil: Mix 2 oz. red pepper flakes and 8 oz. vegetable oil. Soak overnight before using. Any left over can be used for future recipes.

Editor's note: Oil will continue to get hotter as red pepper steeps in it. To keep oil the desired strength, strain out pepper after desired hotness is reached. Hot oil is a traditional Oriental seasoning and may be used in a variety of dishes.

Pat Patterson, Wichita, 1986

Fish Stew

1 lb. frozen fish fillets (sole, haddock or flounder)
1 can (10 ½ oz.) cream of onion soup
1 soup can of water
1 can (16 oz.) tomatoes, drained
1 lemon, sliced thin
2 teaspoons curry powder
1 pkg. (10 to 12 oz.) frozen shrimp, cleaned but not cooked
Salt and pepper
1 tablespoon minced parsley

Fish Stew — continued

Thaw fish at room temperature about 1 hour, then cut into chunks. In soup pot combine onion soup, water, tomatoes, lemon and curry powder; add fish. Bring to simmer and let cook about 20 minutes or until fish flakes. Add shrimp in the last 5 minutes. Season to taste with salt and pepper. Pour into tureen and sprinkle with minced parsley. Makes 3 or 4 servings.

Note: Use cooked shrimp, frozen or canned, if desired.

Patricia Habiger, Spearville, 1985

Pleasant Valley Cheese-Vegetable Soup

    1 cup finely cut celery
    ½ cup finely cut carrot
    ¼ cup finely cut onion
    2 tablespoons instant chicken bouillon
    1 quart water
    1 quart milk
1 ½ lbs. processed American cheese, cubed
    ½ cup butter or margarine
    ½ cup flour
    ½ teaspoon dry mustard
       Salt (optional)

Place celery, carrot, onion, bouillon and water in large saucepan. Cook gently until vegetables are tender. Meanwhile, scald milk in 2-quart pan, but do not boil. Add cheese and stir until melted. Melt butter in small pan. Add flour and mustard; mix until smooth. Stir into cheese-milk mixture and heat. Stir in vegetables and water in which they were cooked. Salt to taste. Serve hot. Makes 2 quarts.

This recipe may be halved. It is a very rich, hearty soup. Better than chicken soup for perking up a puny appetite.

Susan Klingenberg, Wichita, 1989

White Chili

1 lb. white beans
6 cups chicken broth
2 cloves garlic, minced
2 medium onions, chopped (divided)
1 tablespoon oil or margarine
2 cans (4 oz. each) chopped green chilies
2 teaspoons ground cumin
1 ½ teaspoons oregano
¼ teaspoon cayenne pepper
4 cups diced cooked chicken breasts
3 cups grated Monterey Jack cheese

In soup pot combine beans, chicken broth, garlic and half the onions. Bring to boil and simmer until very soft (2½ to 3 hours). More broth made with bouillon may be added. In skillet saute remaining onion until tender. Add chilies and spices. Add to bean mixture. Add diced chicken and simmer 1 hour. Serve topped with grated cheese. Makes 8 to 10 servings.

Note: Instead of cheeese, or in addition to, top white chili with or any of the following: sour cream, chopped ripe olives, chopped tomato, tortilla chips, salsa, guacamole.

Marjorie Parmele, Wichita, 1990

Cream of Chili Soup
(Sopa de Crema de Chile)

3 cans (4 oz. each) green chilies (not jalapenos)
1 can (4 oz.) red chilies (or chopped pimientos)
1 teaspoon baking soda
¾ cup butter or margarine
½ cup chopped onion
¾ cup flour
9 cups milk
1 ½ teaspoons salt

Canned red chilies are hard to find, so pimientos can be substituted with some sacrifice in flavor. Whole chilies should be chopped into ⅜- to ½-inch squares. Place chilies and all their juice into 1-quart bowl. Add baking soda and stir mixture well. Set chilies aside, but stir them occasionally while cream sauce is being prepared. (This is important because chilies are canned with a small amount of citric acid; unless the acid is neutralized with baking soda, the cream sauce may curdle later on when the chilies are added to it.) Melt butter in 2-quart pan. Add chopped onion; saute until it is quite soft, but not brown. Add flour; mash onion with flour and stir until smooth paste is produced. Add milk and salt. Slowly heat mixture to boiling with constant stirring. Boil gently, with stirring, for a minute or two. Stir chili mixture into cream sauce. Makes about 15 servings.

Note: This recipe makes a thick, rich soup. Thinner preparation can be obtained by using smaller quantities of butter and flour. The color of this soup, red and green against a white background, makes it appropriate for inclusion in a menu for the Christmas season. Leftover soup can be stored under refrigeration and reheated as needed.

Robert V. Christian Jr., Wichita, 1981

Portuguese Potato Soup

   2 medium onions, chopped
   1 clove garlic, chopped
   3 tablespoons butter
   4 cups water
1 ½ cups diced cooked ham (about ½ lb.)
   1 can (6 oz.) tomato paste
   1 can (10 ½ oz.) beef consommé
   1 can (15 ½ oz.) red kidney beans (do not drain)
   2 teaspoons salt
  ¼ teaspoon pepper
   1 bay leaf
   3 cups cubed cooked potatoes
    Watercress or chopped parsley (optional)

In a large kettle saute onions and garlic in butter. Add water, ham, tomato paste, consommé, kidney beans, salt, pepper and bay leaf. Bring to boil. Lower heat and simmer uncovered 20 minutes. Add potatoes and cook 10 minutes longer. Pour into soup bowls. Garnish with watercress or parsley, if desired. Makes about 10 1-cup servings.

Nancy Worsham, Wichita, 1978

Hungarian Potato Soup

3 cups diced potatoes
1 cup diced celery
½ cup chopped onion
½ cup diced pimiento
  Salt and pepper to taste
2 cups water
2 tablespoons flour
4 tablespoons butter
4 cups hot milk

In soup pot combine potatoes, celery, onion, pimiento, salt, pepper and water. Cook very slowly until potatoes are tender. In small bowl blend flour and butter, then gradually add some of the hot milk , stirring constantly. Add flour mixture and remainder of hot milk to potatoes and cook 5 minutes longer. Makes 6 to 8 servings.

Mrs. A.D. Kipfer, Wichita, 1956

Creamy Cauliflower Soup

3 teaspoons instant chicken-flavored bouillon, or 3 chicken bouillon cubes
2 cups boiling water
1 pkg. (8 to 10 oz.) frozen cauliflower
8 water chestnuts, sliced
¼ teaspoon lemon and pepper seasoning
1 tablespoon chopped parsley

In soup pot stir instant chicken bouillon in hot water until dissolved. Add cauliflower pieces and simmer just until tender. Process in blender or food processor until smooth. Return to soup pot; add water chestnuts and lemon pepper and reheat. Serve sprinkled with chopped parsley. Makes 4 servings (30 calories per serving).

Billie Denny, Wichita, 1977

Canadian Cheese Soup

1 cup chopped onion
½ cup butter
½ cup flour
2 quarts milk
2 cups chicken or beef stock
1 cup diced carrots
1 cup finely chopped celery
Salt to taste
2 cups cubed sharp cheese
Pepper to taste

In soup pot saute onion, butter and flour, but do not brown. Add milk to thickened onion and flour mixture. Then add stock, carrots and celery; bring to low boil. Cook until vegetables are tender. Salt to taste. Before serving, stir in cheese and pepper to taste. Makes 6 servings.

Katherine Stanley, Wichita, 1975

Salmon Chowder

1 cup diced potatoes
⅓ cup sliced onion
2 cups boiling water
½ teaspoon salt
1 can (7 ¾ oz.) salmon, drained (1 cup)
1 ½ teaspoons butter
¼ cup chopped green pepper
¼ cup light cream

In soup pot combine potatoes, onion, water, salt, salmon, butter and green pepper; cover and simmer about 30 minutes. Remove from heat and stir in cream. Makes 4 servings.

Mrs. Ernest L. Green, Clay Center, 1966

Big Spoon Potato-Cheese Soup

6 slices bacon, cut in small pieces
1 cup finely chopped onion
½ clove garlic, finely chopped
½ cup finely chopped green pepper
2 small tender stalks celery, finely chopped
5 sprigs parsley, finely chopped
1 cup water
2 cups leftover mashed potatoes
2 cups milk
½ teaspoon salt
¼ teaspoon pepper
Cayenne pepper to taste (optional)
1 cup grated American cheese
Croutons

Fry bacon until crisp in soup pot. Remove bacon from pan and drain all drippings, reserving 1 tablespoonful. Using reserved drippings, saute onion, garlic and green pepper in covered kettle until soft, stirring occasionally. Add bacon pieces, celery, parsley and water. Cover kettle and simmer 15 minutes. Add mashed potatoes and steam in covered kettle for about 5 minutes to soften potatoes and prevent lumps. Add milk, salt, pepper and cayenne. Bring to simmer over medium-low heat, stirring constantly. Mash any potato lumps against side of kettle with large spoon. Add cheese, turn off heat and cover kettle. Do not remove lid for 10 minutes. Before serving, stir to mix well. Ladle over croutons in soup bowls. Makes 4 servings.

Mrs. Harold Bauer, Wichita, 1963

MAIN DISHES

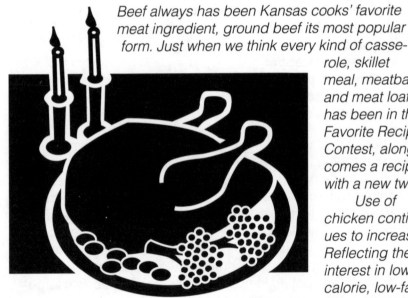

Beef always has been Kansas cooks' favorite meat ingredient, ground beef its most popular form. Just when we think every kind of casserole, skillet meal, meatball and meat loaf has been in the Favorite Recipe Contest, along comes a recipe with a new twist. Use of chicken continues to increase. Reflecting the interest in low-calorie, low-fat foods, few of the recent preparations submitted sport the rich sauces popular in the 1950s. Turkey is everyday fare, instead of being reserved for holidays and large gatherings.

Landlocked Kansans submit only a few contest recipes using fish, and many of them are for canned tuna.

Italian and Mexican accents for meat and poultry are favored, with Oriental-inspired contest entries increasing.

Kansans enjoy the flavor of food cooked outdoors year-round, and they'll barbecue anything — even bologna.

GROUND BEEF

Hamburger Quick Meal

1 ½ lbs. ground beef
4 or 5 medium potatoes, cut in julienne strips
1 large onion, sliced thin to medium
1 small head or ½ head of large cabbage, cut very fine (about 4 cups)
1 teaspoon salt
1 tablespoon pepper
Water

Brown ground beef in extra-large electric skillet; drain. Return ground beef to skillet and add potatoes, onion and cabbage. Add salt and pepper and ¾ cup water. Put lid on skillet and steam 10 minutes on medium heat. Stir. Add more water, ½ cup at a time, and stir as often as necessary. Continue to cook until vegetables are soft. Makes 3 to 4 servings.

This tastes like a bierock mixture and is also low-calorie.

JoNel Lohmeyer, Hays, 1990

Quick and Easy Meat Loaf

2 lbs. hamburger
1 can (15 to 16 oz.) sloppy joe mix
¼ lb. crackers, crushed

In large bowl combine hamburger, sloppy joe mix and crackers. Put in 8x11-inch baking pan or dish. Bake in 325-degree oven approximately 1 hour. Makes 6 to 8 servings.

Years ago I needed a quick and easy meat dish for a Boy Scout cookout. My daughter suggested the above. I generally fix it in a Dutch oven using coals. I have found the boys like sloppy joes, so the flavor hit the spot with the boys in a meat loaf. Also I like mine well-done and crusty so I generally bake longer than suggested.

Elber R. Buller, Wichita, 1989

Poor Man's Filets

2 tablespoons butter or margarine
½ cup onion, chopped
2 tablespoons green pepper, chopped
1 can (4 oz.) mushroom stems and pieces, drained,
  reserve liquid
2 lbs. lean ground beef
½ cup dry bread crumbs
1 teaspoon salt
⅛ teaspoon pepper
¼ teaspoon thyme
⅛ teaspoon oregano
⅛ teaspoon marjoram
  Pinch of ginger
  Pinch of nutmeg
1 teaspoon instant chicken bouillon, mixed with
  reserved mushroom juice
1 lb. bacon

Melt butter in small skillet; saute onion and green pepper in melted butter until clear. Add mushrooms, cover and cook 2 to 3 minutes. Put ground beef in large mixing bowl; add crumbs, salt, pepper, thyme, oregano, marjoram, ginger, nutmeg, bouillon and sauteed vegetables. Mix with hands. Make patties to desired thickness. Wrap bacon around the side of each patty so that it holds the meat firm and fasten with round, wooden toothpick. Put on baking sheet and freeze until solid. Store in boxes or plastic bags. Move from freezer to broiling pan in the morning and store in refrigerator. Broil about 3 inches from heat, 6 to 10 minutes per side (time varies according to desired degree of doneness). To cook frozen patties, brown both sides under broiler, turn broiler off and bake at 350 degrees until as done as you like them. Makes 7 to 10 patties.

These are great for unexpected company or just a busy family day.

Marilee Skidmore, Ellinwood, 1986

Japanese Hamburger

¼ cup blanched, slivered almonds
1 tablespoon butter or margarine
¾ lb. ground beef
1 cup water
¼ teaspoon salt
1 cup fine noodles
1 pkg. (10 oz.) Japanese style vegetables
1 tablespoon soy sauce

In large skillet saute almonds in butter in skillet until lightly browned. Remove from pan and set aside. Brown ground beef well in butter remaining in skillet, leaving meat in chunks. Stir in water and salt and bring to a boil. Stir in noodles. Cover and simmer for 2 minutes. Add vegetables; bring to a full boil over medium heat, separating vegetables with a fork and stirring frequently. Cover and simmer for 3 minutes. Stir in soy sauce and sprinkle with almonds. Makes 4 servings.

Mary Bauer, Wichita, 1989

Meat Loaf

½ cup Grape Nuts cereal
½ cup water
1 lb. ground beef
1 egg, slightly beaten
2 teaspoons Worcestershire sauce
½ cup chopped onion
   Salt and pepper to taste
¼ cup ketchup

In small bowl combine cereal and water; set aside. In large bowl combine ground beef, egg, Worcestershire, onion, salt and pepper; add cereal-water mixture. Put in loaf pan and spread ketchup over top. Bake at 350 degrees for 1 hour. Makes 6 servings.

Pearl Butts, Wichita, 1990

Individual Lemon Beefies

1 ½ lbs. ground chuck or round
2 tablespoons lemon juice
1 tablespoon water
⅓ cup fresh bread crumbs
¼ teaspoon salt
¼ teaspoon pepper
½ teaspoon meat tenderizer
Sauce
⅓ cup ketchup
¼ teaspoon prepared mustard
⅛ teaspoon ground cloves
¼ teaspoon steak sauce
1 tablespoon lemon juice
¼ teaspoon salt
Lemon slices for garnish

In large mixing bowl combine beef, lemon juice, water, bread crumbs, salt, pepper and meat tenderizer; mix thoroughly. Shape into six individual loaves (3x2x1 inches). Place in a shallow baking dish and bake 5 minutes in a 450-degree oven.

In small mixing bowl combine ketchup, mustard, cloves, steak sauce, lemon juice and salt.

Remove meat loaves from oven. Spoon sauce over loaves and return to oven for 10 to 20 minutes. Remove from oven and place thin slices of lemon on top of loaves. Makes 6 servings.

Note: Those who prefer beef well-done may want to extend the initial cooking time 5 to 10 minutes.

Elaine Davis, Wichita, 1976

Meat Loaf Italian Style

- **1 cup medium cracker crumbs (20 crackers)**
- **1 ½ lbs. ground beef**
- **1 can (6 oz.) tomato paste**
- **2 eggs**
- **1 medium onion, finely chopped**
- **¼ cup finely chopped green pepper**
- **¾ teaspoon salt**
- **Dash pepper**
- **1 carton (12 oz.) small-curd cottage cheese**
- **1 can (3 oz.) broiled mushrooms, drained and chopped**
- **1 tablespoon snipped parsley**
- **¼ teaspoon oregano**

Set aside ½ cup cracker crumbs. In large mixing bowl combine remaining crumbs with beef, tomato paste, eggs, onion, green pepper, salt and pepper. Pat half of the mixture in the bottom of an 8x8x2-inch baking pan. Combine reserved crumbs, cottage cheese, mushrooms, parsley and oregano. Spread evenly over meat in pan. Top with remaining meat mixture. Bake in 350-degree oven 1 hour. Let stand about 5 minutes before cutting into squares. Makes 6 to 8 servings.

Margaret Blackwell, Augusta, 1966

Tamale Bake

1 ½ lbs. ground beef
1 cup chopped onions
1 clove garlic, minced
½ cup diced green pepper
2 ½ cups canned tomatoes
1 can (12 oz.) whole kernel corn, undrained
1 ½ tablespoons chili powder
1 tablespoon salt
¼ teaspoon pepper
½ cup yellow cornmeal
1 cup water
Cheese Cornmeal Topping
1 ½ cups milk
1 teaspoon salt
2 tablespoons butter
½ cup yellow cornmeal
1 cup shredded cheddar cheese
2 eggs, lightly beaten

In 12-inch skillet, lightly cook meat. Add onions, garlic and green pepper. Cook and stir until onion is golden. Stir in tomatoes, corn, chili powder, salt and pepper. Simmer 5 minutes. In small bowl mix cornmeal and water; stir into meat mixture. Cover; simmer about 8 minutes.

For topping: Meanwhile, in medium saucepan heat milk with salt and butter. Slowly stir in cornmeal. Cook, stirring constantly, until thickened. Remove from heat; stir in cheese and eggs.

Turn meat mixture into 3-quart casserole. Spread evenly with topping. Bake in 375-degree oven 30 to 40 minutes or until bubbling hot. Makes 8 servings.

Alice Gerbitz, Wichita, 1964

Easy Stroganoff Bake

1 ½ lbs. ground beef
1 medium onion, chopped
2 tablespoons parsley flakes
½ teaspoon garlic powder
1 teaspoon salt
½ teaspoon pepper
1 can (7 oz.) mushrooms, drained
1 can (10 ½ oz.) minestrone soup
1 cup sour cream
½ cup milk
1 teaspoon poppy seeds
Biscuit Topping
1 ½ cups flour
2 teaspoons baking powder
1 teaspoon paprika
½ teaspoon salt
½ teaspoon celery seed
¼ teaspoon pepper
¼ cup shortening
¾ cup milk
Poppy seed

In large skillet brown beef with onion, parsley flakes and garlic powder. Stir in salt, pepper, mushrooms and soup. Simmer 15 minutes. Blend in sour cream and milk. Heat thoroughly. Place in a 9x9-inch baking dish or 2-quart casserole.

Into medium bowl sift flour, baking powder, paprika and salt. Add celery seed and pepper. Cut in shortening until particles are fine. Add milk. Stir only until dry particles are moistened.

Drop biscuit mixture by tablespoonfuls onto meat mixture. Sprinkle with poppy seed. Bake in 475-degree oven 15 to 20 minutes. Makes 6 to 8 servings.

Mrs. Joe E. Hummer, Chanute, 1965

Sweet-Sour Meatballs

1 lb. ground beef
1 ½ teaspoons salt
¼ teaspoon pepper
1 can (5 oz.) water chestnuts, thinly sliced
1 cup milk
¼ cup flour
¼ cup butter or margarine
2 tablespoons cornstarch
½ cup sugar
¼ cup wine vinegar
1 tablespoon soy sauce
1 medium green pepper, chopped
1 can (16 oz.) pineapple cubes or tidbits, undrained

In mixing bowl combine beef, salt, pepper, water chestnuts and milk. Form into meatballs; roll in flour and cook in frying pan in butter over medium heat, turning until all sides are brown and meatballs are cooked through. In saucepan combine cornstarch, sugar, vinegar, soy sauce, green pepper, pineapple and pineapple juice; bring to a boil. Reduce heat and cook about 5 minutes. Pour over meatballs. Serve hot. Makes 6 to 8 servings.

Mrs. H.M. Moses, Wichita, 1958

BEEF

Spicy Brisket

4 to 6 lbs. beef brisket
Allspice
5 beef bouillon cubes
Cornstarch-water paste

Place brisket, fat side up, on rack on broiler pan. Fill pan with water. Generously sprinkle fat side of brisket with allspice until it is covered. Bake 6 hours at 275 degrees. Remove from oven, wrap brisket in foil and place in refrigerator until thoroughly chilled. Pour juice into saucepan and refrigerate. Slice chilled brisket ¼ inch thick across grain and layer in baking dish. Skim chilled fat from juice, heat juice to boiling, reduce heat and add 5 beef bouillon cubes and thicken with cornstarch-water paste. Pour gravy over meat and bake 1 hour in 350-degree oven.

Janice Abney, Newton, 1982

Dilly Pot Roast

4 to 5 lbs. chuck roast
Liquid smoke
Fat from chuck or oil
Coarse black pepper
Dill seed
Beer

Rub both sides of chuck roast with liquid smoke. In skillet, render fat and discard or heat oil; brown meat on all sides. Place in casserole; sprinkle liberally with ground black pepper and dill seed. Pour about 1 cup beer over meat. Cover; bake in preheated 300-degree oven 3 to 4 hours or until beef is tender. Remove meat to platter and carve; pass beer sauce. Makes 6 to 8 servings.

Betty Reed, Ellis, 1972

Pepper Steak

1 lb. round steak
¼ cup cooking oil
1 teaspoon salt
Dash of pepper
¼ cup finely diced onion
1 clove garlic
3 large green peppers, cut into 1-inch pieces
1 cup sliced celery
1 cup beef bouillon
2 tablespoons cornstarch
¼ cup cold water
2 teaspoons soy sauce

Cut steak diagonally into thin slices, then cut slices into 2-inch pieces. Preheat frying pan over medium heat. Add oil, salt and pepper. When oil is hot, add meat and cook until brown, stirring frequently. Turn heat to low; add onion, garlic, green pepper, celery and bouillon. Cover and cook until vegetables are crisply tender, about 10 minutes. (Add hot water, if necessary.) Blend cornstarch, cold water and soy sauce; add to meat mixture and cook until thickened, stirring constantly, about 5 minutes. Makes 4 servings.

Leona A. Rossilon, Wichita, 1958

Estofado With Beer Rice

1 ½ lbs. lean beef stew meat
1 large onion, chopped
1 garlic clove, minced
4 tablespoons olive oil
3 tablespoons vinegar
1 can (7 oz.) green chili salsa
½ cup tomato sauce
1 cup red wine
1 bay leaf
1 teaspoon oregano
   Salt and pepper to taste
Beer Rice
1 tablespoon olive oil
1 cup rice
1 can (10 ½ oz.) French onion soup
1 soup can beer

In large saucepan combine beef, onion, garlic, oil, vinegar, salsa, tomato sauce, wine, bay leaf, oregano, salt and pepper. Cover, bring to a boil; reduce heat and simmer 2 hours or until meat is tender.

Heat oil in medium skillet; add rice and brown, stirring carefully. Add soup and beer. Cover pan and cook over medium heat 20 to 25 minutes.

Serve estofado over rice. Makes 4 to 6 servings.

Celinda Black, Wichita, 1974

Ho-Gar Roast Beef

2 ½ teaspoons salt
½ teaspoon pepper
2 ½ oz. horseradish
¾ oz. garlic juice
1 5-lb. beef rump roast

In small bowl mix salt, pepper, horseradish and garlic juice; spread over roast. Place in a plastic bag or tight container. Place in refrigerator and marinate 24 hours. Remove to baking dish and roast in 350-degree oven 3 hours or until it reaches desired doneness. Makes 8 to 10 servings.

Mrs. J.L. Lenhart, Goddard, 1975

CHICKEN

Good and Easy Chicken

8 chicken breast halves
1 jar (18 oz.) apricot preserves
1 bottle (8 oz.) Russian dressing
1 envelope dry onion soup mix

Skin chicken (use boneless if preferred) and place in single layer in 9x13-inch baking dish. Combine preserves, dressing and onion soup mix; spread over chicken, cover and marinate in refrigerator overnight. Bake, uncovered, at 350 degrees for 1 hour. Baste occasionally with sauce. Makes 6 to 8 servings.

Served over rice and accompanied by a veggie and a fruit salad, you have a good company dinner or an easy family supper.

Susan Humphrey, Wichita, 1989

Chicken Ranchero Spaghetti

1 pkg. (10 oz.) spaghetti
1 broiler-fryer chicken, cooked, deboned and cubed
1 can (10 ¾ oz.) cream of mushroom soup
½ cup milk
1 can (3 oz.) chopped green chilies
6 slices American cheese

Cook spaghetti according to package directions. Meanwhile, in large bowl mix chicken, soup, milk and chilies. Chop cheese slices and add to chicken mixture, stirring to blend. Thoroughly drain spaghetti and add to chicken mixture, mixing well. Turn into large casserole. Bake in 350-degree oven 15 minutes. Makes 4 to 6 servings.

Marla Duncan, Wichita, 1983

Light Chicken Florentine

 1 broiler-fryer chicken (2 ½ to 3 lbs.), quartered
  Salt and pepper
 2 tablespoons low-calorie Italian-style French dressing
 1 can (4 oz.) mushroom slices
 ¼ cup flour
1 ½ cups skim milk
 ¼ teaspoon salt
  A few grains pepper
 ¾ teaspoon seasoned salt
 1 chicken bouillon cube
 2 pkgs. (10 oz. each) frozen chopped spinach, cooked
  and drained
 4 tablespoons grated Parmesan cheese

 Sprinkle chicken with salt and pepper. Place skin side down on rack in broiler pan; brush lightly with some of the French dressing. Place in oven 5 to 6 inches from heat. Broil 20 to 25 minutes; turn and brush with remaining dressing and meat juices from pan. Broil an additional 20 to 25 minutes, or until fork-tender. While chicken is broiling, prepare sauce. Drain mushrooms and reserve liquid. In a saucepan mix flour and liquid from mushrooms. Gradually add skim milk and beat with a whisk to blend. Cook over moderate heat (about 250 degrees), stirring constantly until thickened. Add ¼ teaspoon salt, pepper, seasoned salt and bouillon cube. Stir over moderately low heat (about 225 degrees) until bouillon cube is dissolved. Add mushrooms. Spoon well-drained spinach into a heat-proof baking dish. Arrange chicken over spinach. Top with mushroom sauce and Parmesan cheese. Broil 3 to 4 inches from heat 3 to 5 minutes. Makes 4 servings.
 A dish I created for the light and lively.

Lola Cleavinger, Wichita, 1985

Baked Chicken Breasts

8 chicken breast halves
8 slices bacon
1 pkg. (3 oz.) dried beef, shredded
1 can (10 ¾ oz.) cream of mushroom soup
1 cup sour cream

Bone and skin each breast. Roll each breast and wrap with bacon; fasten with toothpick. Sprinkle dried chipped beef in the bottom of an 8- or 9-inch square baking dish. Lay chicken breasts on top of beef. Blend mushroom soup and sour cream and pour over breasts. Bake 4 hours in 275-degree oven. Cover with foil all but last hour. Makes 4 to 6 servings.

Note: There is enough sauce to accommodate as many as 12 chicken breast halves, but sauce servings will be smaller.

Patricia Miller, Wichita, 1973

Chicken Squares

3 to 4 cups cooked, chopped chicken
3 cups broth
9 slices day-old bread, torn into bite-size pieces
½ cup chopped pimiento
2 tablespoons chopped onion
1 teaspoon salt
Pepper to taste
4 eggs, well beaten

Cook one large stewing chicken in enough water to make 3 cups broth. When chicken is tender, remove meat from bones and cube. In large mixing bowl combine chicken, broth, bread, pimiento, onion, salt, pepper and eggs; mix well. Add well-beaten eggs and stir. Pour into a well-greased 13x9½-inch pan. Bake 1 hour in a 325-degree oven. Cut into squares to serve. Makes 9 to 12 servings.

Mrs. Charlie Harant, Bluff City, 1962

Old-Fashioned Chicken and Dumplings

1 (4- or 5-lb.) chicken (3 small broiler-fryers may be substituted)
Water
Salt
1 large onion, sliced
1 cup celery tops or sliced celery stalks
1 carrot, sliced
8 crushed peppercorns
1 bay leaf
2 cups flour
1 teaspoon salt
3 teaspoons baking powder
6 tablespoons chicken fat
¾ cup milk

Place chicken in a large pot and cover with water and enough salt so that the water is barely salty to the taste. Add onion, celery, carrot, peppercorns and bay leaf. Cook over low heat until chicken falls from the bones. Remove all the meat from the pot and set aside. Cook bones and skin about 2 hours longer, or until broth is concentrated and quite rich. Skim fat from surface of broth and chill. Strain broth and mix with chicken meat in pan; heat to boiling. Sift flour, salt and baking powder into mixing bowl. When chicken fat has hardened, cut into flour mixture with two knives in a crisscross motion. (Lard or other shortening may be added if there is not enough chicken fat.) Stir in milk; drop mixture by the spoonful onto surface of broth. Cover pan tightly and simmer 12 to 15 minutes. Makes 6 to 8 servings.

Mrs. Glenn Dunne Jr., Wichita, 1961

Chinese Diced Chicken and Almonds

2 lbs. chicken breasts
2 tablespoons shortening
¾ cup blanched almonds
½ cup chopped celery
3 green onions, cut into 1/2-inch pieces
1 small piece fresh ginger
1 cup chicken broth or consommé
1 teaspoon salt
¼ teaspoon pepper (preferably freshly ground)
¼ teaspoon sugar
2 tablespoons cornstarch
2 tablespoons water
1 tablespoon soy sauce
Cooked rice

Cut chicken into 1-inch squares and refrigerate until ready to cook. Heat electric frying pan to 350 degrees. Add shortening; brown nuts on both sides. Remove from pan and drain on absorbent paper; reserve for later use. Add chicken to pan and saute lightly on both sides so it loses its raw color but does not brown. In small bowl combine celery, onions, ginger, chicken broth, salt, pepper and sugar. Pour combined ingredients into frying pan. Reduce heat to 200 degrees, cover pan and cook until chicken is tender, about 20 minutes. In small bowl mix cornstarch, water and soy sauce; add to mixture in pan. Continue cooking until sauce thickens; add browned nuts and serve on hot cooked rice. Makes 4 to 6 servings.

Betty Bogue, Wichita, 1961

Slim Jim Baked Chicken

4 chicken legs or thighs (or any pieces of chicken desired)
1 teaspoon garlic salt
2 teaspoons paprika
½ teaspoon oregano, crushed
½ teaspoon fresh grated lemon peel
½ cup fresh lemon juice
½ cup water
Snipped parsley (for garnish)

Season chicken pieces with garlic salt, rubbing well into flesh. Sprinkle with paprika. Place in shallow baking pan, skin side down. In small bowl combine oregano, lemon peel, lemon juice and water; pour over chicken. Bake uncovered at 400 degrees about 40 minutes. Turn chicken and continue baking until done, about 35 minutes, basting with pan drippings once or twice. Garnish with snipped parsley, if desired. Makes 4 servings.

Carolyn M. Ramsey, Wichita, 1978

Old Southern Buttermilk Baked Chicken

¾ cup buttermilk
1 chicken, cut up for frying
¾ cup flour
1 ½ teaspoons salt
¼ teaspoon pepper
¼ cup butter or margarine
¾ cup buttermilk
1 can (10 ¾ oz.) cheddar cheese soup (or cream of mushroom soup)
1 soup can water

Place ¾ cup buttermilk in bowl. Dip pieces of chicken in buttermilk. In another bowl combine flour, salt and pepper; roll chicken pieces in flour mixture. Melt butter in a 13x9x2-inch pan. Place chicken pieces in pan and bake uncovered in 425-degree oven 30 minutes. Blend remaining buttermilk with cheddar cheese soup and water. Pour over chicken and bake another 15 minutes or until tender. Makes 4 to 6 servings.

Mrs J.A. Patterson, Newton, 1968

Vietnamese Sweet Chicken

1 chicken, cut up (about 2 lbs.)
   Oil
1 clove garlic
2 ½ tablespoons brown sugar
1 teaspoon salt
1 tablespoon fish sauce or soy sauce
¼ cup water

Brown chicken in oil in large frying pan. In a bowl, crush garlic; add brown sugar, salt, fish sauce or soy sauce, and water; stir. Drain excess oil from chicken; pour garlic mixture over chicken in frying pan. Cover and cook over medium heat, turning chicken occasionally. Chicken is done when tender to the fork and covered with syrup-like coating. Makes 4 to 5 servings.

Huong Thi Butler, Wichita, 1975

EGGS

Egg Souffle — Irish Style

1 tablespoon butter or margarine
1 can (14 ¾ oz.) spaghetti in tomato sauce
6 large eggs
½ cup milk
Salt and pepper if desired

Preheat oven to 375 degrees. Butter bottom and sides of 1-quart casserole dish. Empty spaghetti into casserole and spread evenly over bottom. In separate bowl beat eggs, milk, salt and pepper. Pour over spaghetti. Bake in preheated oven approximately 45 minutes, checking occasionally as oven temperatures may vary. Remove when egg has risen and cooked. (Make sure that dish is not removed while egg is still runny.) It should be golden brown. Makes 4 servings.

Charlotte Lamb, Wichita, 1983

Western Curried Eggs

6 hard-cooked eggs
2 tablespoons butter or margarine
2 tablespoons minced onion
2 tablespoons flour
1 teaspoon curry powder
2 cups milk
1 teaspoon salt
¼ teaspoon pepper
2 teaspoons grated orange rind
¼ cup orange juice
3 cups hot fluffy rice
Parsley (for garnish)

Shell and quarter eggs; set aside. Melt butter in skillet; saute onion until tender. Stir in flour and curry powder and cook until bubbly. Stir in milk. Cook until thickened, stirring constantly. Add salt, pepper, orange rind and juice, then eggs. Heat, stirring gently to avoid breaking eggs. Spoon over rice; garnish with parsley. Makes 4 to 6 servings.

Vere Grimsman, Haven, 1961

Baked Eggs

3 tablespoons butter
2 medium onions, thinly sliced
Salt and pepper
4 eggs
2 tablespoons fine dry bread crumbs
4 slices processed sharp American cheese

Preheat oven to 350 degrees. Melt butter in skillet; add onions and cook about 5 minutes or until just tender. Spread onions in an 8-inch pie plate; sprinkle lightly with salt and pepper. Break eggs over onions; sprinkle with salt and pepper, then with crumbs. Top with cheese slices. Bake in preheated oven, uncovered, 10 to 15 minutes or until eggs are firm. Makes 4 servings.

Mrs. Phillip Aaron, Wichita, 1956

Swiss Eggs

1 large onion
¼ lb. processed Swiss cheese
6 slices bacon
6 eggs
½ teaspoon salt
⅛ teaspoon pepper

Peel onion and cut into thin slices. Cut cheese into thin slices. Cut bacon strips into thirds, then fry in skillet until crisp. Pour off all but 1 tablespoon bacon fat. Break the eggs over bacon slices in skillet. Place cheese slices over eggs. Add onion slices, salt and pepper. Cover skillet and cook gently 5 minutes or until eggs have set and cheese has melted. Makes 4 servings.

Capt. Jay H. Quick, Shilling AFB, 1957

Mexican Scrambled Eggs

2 tablespoons minced onion
1 small green pepper, diced
½ clove garlic, minced (optional)
1 tablespoon butter
⅓ cup condensed tomato soup
6 eggs, slightly beaten
Salt to taste

In skillet saute onion, green pepper and garlic in butter until golden brown. Add tomato soup and cook about 3 minutes to blend the flavors. Add eggs and salt and stir lightly as the eggs become firm. Serve while hot. Makes 4 servings.

Josie Vaughn, Fredonia, 1962

Kiowa Eggs

4 slices sandwich bread
2 tablespoons butter, melted
4 eggs
¼ teaspoon salt
Dash of black pepper
⅛ teaspoon thyme
4 tablespoons light cream
1 tablespoon butter, melted
4 tablespoons grated cheese
4 tablespoons barbecue sauce
8 stuffed olives

Trim crusts from bread; toast slices and brush lightly with melted butter. Place toast on greased cookie sheet or heat-proof platter. Break eggs into mixing bowl and beat lightly. Add salt, pepper, thyme, cream and butter to eggs and beat again. Pour into greased skillet and cook slowly, tipping skillet so liquid will flow to the sides and solidify. When eggs are firm but still moist, pile equal portions on toast slices. Sprinkle 1 tablespoon cheese on each portion and top with a dribble of barbecue sauce. Bake in 425-degree oven 5 minutes or until cheese is melted and golden. Garnish with thin slices of stuffed olives. Serve at once with french fried potatoes and green tossed salad. Makes 4 servings.

Fenton Fly, Wichita, 1959

FISH AND SEAFOOD

Easy Baked Fish

Non-stick spray
1 ½ lbs. white fish fillets (frozen)
1 cup light mayonnaise
1 teaspoon seasoning salt
½ to 1 teaspoon chopped parsley

Spray 9x13-inch baking dish with non-stick spray. Place frozen fish fillets in pan. Spread each portion with ¼ to ½ inch of mayonnaise to cover top. Sprinkle with seasoning salt and parsley. In 350-degree oven, bake for 15 to 20 minutes covered with foil, then uncover and continue to bake for 5 to 10 minutes to lightly brown. Makes 4 to 6 servings.

Can also be baked in the microwave in about 8 to 10 minutes.

Pat Martin, Haysville, 1988

Perfection Fish Bake

1 lb. fillets of sole (if frozen, must be thawed)
1 can (3 oz.) sliced mushrooms
3 tablespoons lemon juice
1 tablespoon water
1 tablespoon parsley flakes or chopped fresh parsley
½ teaspoon dry mustard
½ teaspoon salt
¼ teaspoon pepper

Dry fillets of sole with paper toweling. Place fillets in greased 2½-quart shallow baking dish. Top fillets with mushrooms. In small bowl mix lemon juice, water, parsley, mustard, salt and pepper; pour over fillets and mushrooms. Cover and bake in a 375-degree oven about 25 minutes or until fish flakes. Makes 4 servings.

Note: Other lean fillets of fish may be substituted for sole, such as halibut, haddock or cod.

Mrs. V. E. Schoonover, Eureka, 1969

Fish Casserole (Microwave)

2 cups canned salmon
1 ½ cups grated Swiss cheese
1 egg
Salt and pepper to taste
3 tablespoons butter, melted (divided use)
¼ cup bread crumbs

Flake salmon. In medium bowl mix with grated cheese. Add the egg and mix well. Add salt, pepper and 1 tablespoon melted butter; mix well. Line 8x11-inch dish with parchment paper or spray with a non-stick coating; spoon in salmon mixture. Add 2 tablespoons butter to crumbs in small bowl and mix well; sprinkle over top of casserole mixture; bake in microwave oven 7 minutes. Remove from oven and let stand 5 minutes. Makes 4 servings.

Mrs. George Herrmann, Dodge City, 1975

Rice and Tuna Casserole

1 can (6½ to 7 oz.) tuna
½ cup raw rice
½ cup grated onion
½ cup grated carrot
¼ teaspoon curry powder
1 egg, beaten
1 can (10 ¾ oz.) cream of mushroom soup
1 soup can water

In large mixing bowl combine tuna, rice, onion, carrot, curry powder and egg. Blend soup and water in a small saucepan. Heat to boiling; pour into tuna mixture and mix well. Pour into a 1½-quart casserole and bake in 350-degree oven 50 to 60 minutes. Makes 4 generous servings.

Irene Laughlin, Wichita, 1967

Wild Rice Casserole

1 cup white rice
1 cup wild rice
2 medium onions, chopped
2 cans (2 oz. each) mushrooms
½ green pepper, chopped
2 cups finely diced celery
3 tablespoons butter
3 cans (7 oz. each) shrimp
1 large can crabmeat
1 pimiento, chopped
2 cans (10 ¾ oz. each) cream of mushroom soup
White sauce
¼ cup slivered blanched almonds

Cook and drain both white and wild rice according to package directions. In large skillet saute onions, mushrooms, green pepper and celery in butter. Add to rice in large mixing bowl with shrimp, crab and pimiento. Pour into greased casserole or 9x13x2-inch baking dish. Pour mushroom soup over all. Mix lightly. Bake 45 minutes in 350-degree oven. Serve with rich white sauce and slivered almonds. Makes 12 to 15 servings.

Marilyn Savonen, Wichita, 1968

Spaghetti Siciliano

½ **stick butter**
½ **cup olive or vegetable oil**
1 **clove garlic, quartered**
  Peel of 1 lemon
¼ **cup minced parsley**
1 **bottle clam juice**
2 **cans minced clams**
  Juice of 1 lemon
  Cooked spaghetti (do not overcook)

In large skillet melt butter and olive oil together. Add garlic and lemon peel; saute over medium-low heat. Remove peel and garlic when they begin to brown. Add parsley, clam juice, clams and lemon juice; heat slowly until sauce comes to a boil. Serve immediately over cooked spaghetti. Makes 4 servings.

Mrs. Kenneth Hanes, Peabody, 1966

PORK

Jeff's Pork Chops

    4 pork loin chops, center cut
    1 cup sweet vermouth
    ½ cup water
    2 small cloves garlic, crushed
    ½ teaspoon Worcestershire sauce
    1 teaspoon dry mustard
    1 teaspoon fresh or dried basil
    ½ teaspoon fresh or dried marjoram
    1 teaspoon freshly grated orange peel
      Prepared wild rice
      Prepared vegetables

On a grill, quickly sear the pork chops until lightly browned. Remove to a platter. In skillet mix vermouth, water, crushed garlic, Worcestershire sauce, mustard, basil, marjoram and orange peel; bring to a gentle simmer. Place pork chops and juices in skillet, cover and simmer 20 to 25 minutes, turning meat several times. Remove pork chops to a heated platter, increase heat to high and boil to reduce the remaining sauce by half. Arrange pork chops on serving plates with wild rice and a vegetable, such as glazed baby carrots or fresh asparagus. Drizzle remaining sauce over each pork chop and the rice. Makes 4 servings.

A miserable, sleety night in January caused dinner plans with friends to be canceled, so we made this recipe up from scratch with what we had in the house. It has proven to be tremendously popular with family and friends.

Jeffrey and Julie Kimpton, Wichita, 1986

Holiday Pickled Ham

    1 whole, precooked ham, 8 to 12 lbs.
1 ½ cups sherry
    1 cup sugar
    ¾ cup vinegar
    1 tablespoon dry mustard
    1 tablespoon bruised fennel seeds
    2 teaspoons powdered cloves or whole cloves
Or
    ½ precooked ham, 4 to 6 lbs.
    ¾ cup sherry
    ½ cup sugar
    ¾ cup vinegar
1 ½ teaspoons dry mustard
1 ½ teaspoons bruised fennel seeds
    1 teaspoon powdered cloves or whole cloves

Pierce ham with a fine-bladed knife at intervals of about 2 to 3 inches. This allows the marinade to penetrate. Bruise fennel seed in a mortar with a pestle to release the flavor. Stud ham with whole cloves about every 1½ inches. Put ham in a large non-aluminum bowl deep enough to hold the marinade. Add sherry, sugar, vinegar, mustard, fennel and powdered cloves. (Only add powdered cloves if not studding ham with whole cloves). Fill with water until ham is covered. Put in refrigerator and marinate 24 to 48 hours. Put ham and marinade in a large kettle and simmer on low heat 2 to 3 hours. Ham can be prepared ahead and frozen or served at this point. I usually bake the ham at 325 degrees for 1½ to 2 hours on the day it is to be used. This improves the texture. Slice and serve cold. (Remove whole cloves before slicing.) Makes 12 to 24 servings.

I usually buy hams on sale and freeze or pickle them in advance. It stores well.

Catherine L. McKern, Wichita, 1985

Sausage, Spaghetti, Cabbage Stir-Fry

8 oz. uncooked spaghetti
1 lb. pork sausage (bulk Italian sausage best)
4 cups thinly sliced cabbage
1 medium onion, coarsely chopped
1 medium apple, thinly sliced or chopped
2 cloves garlic, minced
1 jar (2 oz.) sliced pimiento
¼ teaspoon red pepper
¼ teaspoon ground sage
1 teaspoon salt
1 ½ cups (6 oz.) shredded Monterey Jack cheese
1 ½ cups (6 oz.) shredded sharp cheddar cheese

Prepare spaghetti according to package instructions. Drain and set aside. In extra-large skillet or wok (at least 12 inches), cook sausage over medium heat until brown. Drain and discard all but 2 tablespoons fat. Add cabbage, onion, apple and garlic; stir-fry over moderate heat until crisp-tender. Stir in pimiento, red pepper, sage and salt. Add spaghetti and stir-fry until hot. Remove from heat and add cheeses. Stir until well mixed. Serve hot. Leftovers refrigerate well. Makes 4 to 6 servings.

I got this recipe from my mother, years ago, before "stir-fry" became popular. It is an excellent "all in one" type stir-fry, with the meat, vegetable, pasta and fruit included. Many people are at first surprised with the combo of spaghetti, sausage and apple but become real believers after the first try.

Bob Sayre, Wichita, 1990

Sweet Country Ribs

4 lbs. country-style pork ribs
1 bottle (2-liter) cola
1 bottle (18 oz.) hickory smoke, onion bits barbecue
sauce
1 cup packed brown sugar

Put ribs in 6-quart Dutch oven with cola and boil 2 hours, or until tender. Drain. Mix barbecue sauce and brown sugar in a separate bowl until smooth. Place ribs in a single layer on a piece of heavy-duty aluminum foil, shiny side up. Pour sauce over ribs. Wrap and seal ribs in foil. Wrap in another piece of foil, shiny side in. They can be refrigerated 24 hours. Bake in the foil at 400 degrees for 45 minutes or until you can hear the sauce bubbling. To serve, slide the foil packet onto a platter and cut open with a knife. Makes 6 servings.

Variation: Place foil packet on hot grill for the same amount of time. I make these in the summer for family dinners. I make them ahead of time, then put them on the grill and serve with potato salad. The meat is real tender and slightly sweet. Cleanup is a breeze!

Debbie Grindstaff, Sedgwick, 1989

Sesame Pork Tenderloin

1 cup chicken stock
¼ cup soy sauce
¼ cup honey
2 tablespoons cooking sherry
1 tablespoon lemon juice
1 clove garlic, minced
1 teaspoon cinnamon
1 teaspoon salt
¼ teaspoon ginger
3 pork tenderloins
2 tablespoon cornstarch
2 tablespoons sesame seeds

In shallow non-aluminum container combine stock, soy sauce, honey, sherry, lemon juice, garlic, cinnamon, salt and ginger. Marinate tenderloins in mixture 2 to 3 hours at room temperature, turning frequently; drain liquid and save. Roll meat in cornstarch and place in 9x13-inch baking dish. Sprinkle with sesame seeds. Bake in 300-degree oven 2 to 2 ½ hours, basting often with reserved marinade. Makes 5 or 6 servings.

Patricia Cue, Wichita, 1984

Ham Steak Baked With Port

1 slice ham
½ cup brown sugar
4 tablespoons prepared mustard
¾ cup port wine
Watercress (for garnish)

Rub both sides of a fairly thick slice of ham with brown sugar. Coat both sides with prepared mustard. Place prepared ham in baking dish and add wine. Bake in 350-degree oven about 1 hour, basting occasionally with the wine. Remove ham to deep, hot platter; skim off fat and pour a little more port into pan if necessary. Stir well and pour sauce over ham. Garnish with watercress. Makes 4 to 5 servings.

Marie S. Johnson, Wichita, 1967

Oven Chop Suey

- ¾ **lb. pork steak, cubed**
- 1 **cup chopped onion**
- 1 **cup chopped celery**
- ¼ **cup uncooked rice**
- ½ **cup water**
- 1 ½ **tablespoons soy sauce**
- 1 **can (10 ¾ oz.) golden mushroom soup**
- 1 **can (8 oz.) bean sprouts**
- **Buttered crumbs**

In large skillet brown pork until tender; add onion and celery and saute for a few minutes longer. Add rice, water, soy sauce, mushroom soup and bean sprouts. Turn into greased casserole. Top mixture with buttered crumbs. Bake for 1½ hours In 350-degree oven. Makes 2 to 3 servings.

Jeannette Coble, Winfield, 1979

Pork Tenderloin Javanese

2 lbs. pork tenderloin
6 Brazil nuts, grated
1 cup minced onion
2 cloves garlic, minced
¼ cup lemon juice
¼ cup soy sauce
2 tablespoons brown sugar
2 tablespoons ground coriander
¼ teaspoon crushed red pepper
¼ cup olive oil or vegetable oil
  Hot curried rice

Trim excess fat from meat. Cut meat into 1-inch cubes. In small bowl combine nuts, onion, garlic, lemon juice, soy sauce, brown sugar, coriander, red pepper and oil. Add pork cubes; marinate 20 minutes. Place pork on metal skewers; reserve marinade. Grill over coals about 10 minutes on each side, brushing once on each side with reserved marinade. Serve on skewers with hot curried rice. Makes 6 servings.

Mrs. Rod Wakeland, Wichita, 1963

MISCELLANEOUS

Veal Paprikash

1 ½ lbs. veal steak
Salt and pepper
Flour
2 tablespoons fat
2 teaspoons paprika
3 onions, sliced
½ cup sour cream
Water (if necessary)

Cut veal into serving pieces. Season with salt and pepper and coat lightly with flour. In skillet heat fat, paprika and onions; saute until onions are limp and transparent. Add meat and brown. Add sour cream and cover. Cook slowly until meat is tender. Add a little water if sauce thickens too much. Serve hot. Makes 4 to 6 servings.

Richard Batchelor, Wichita, 1958

Crockpot Hot Dog Casserole

2 cups peeled and sliced red apples
1 can (16 oz.) sweet potatoes, sliced
1 pkg. wieners, sliced
½ cup brown sugar
1 lemon rind, grated
½ teaspoon salt
½ teaspoon cinnamon
¼ teaspoon nutmeg

Mix half of apples, potatoes and wieners in a greased slow cooker. Combine brown sugar, lemon rind, salt, cinnamon and nutmeg. Spread half of sugar mixture over apple mixture. Repeat layers. Slow-cook 5 to 9 hours. Makes 4 to 6 servings.

Ruth Ann Barr, Pratt, 1976

Teen Bean Bake

        2 cans (20 oz. each) baked beans or pork and beans
        ½ cup ketchup
        1 tablespoon prepared mustard
        ½ lb. frankfurters, cut into 1/2-inch slices
        ¾ cup sifted flour
        1 teaspoon salt
        1 tablespoon sugar
    1 ½ teaspoons baking powder
        ⅔ cup cornmeal
        1 egg
        ⅔ cup plus 2 tablespoons milk
        ¼ cup butter, melted
        ⅓ cup chopped onion

In bowl mix beans, ketchup, mustard and frankfurters; turn into buttered baking dish. Prepare corn bread topping by sifting into a bowl the flour, salt, sugar, baking powder and cornmeal. In small bowl beat egg slightly; add milk, melted butter and chopped onion. Combine with dry ingredients, stirring only until moist. Spoon on top of bean mixture. Bake in 400-degree oven 35 to 40 minutes. Makes 7 servings.

Lester Donaldson, Derby, 1958

Fondue Welsh Rabbit

        ¼ cup butter or margaine
        ¼ cup flour
        ½ teaspoon salt
        ¼ teaspoon pepper
        ¼ teaspoon dry mustard
        ¼ teaspoon Worcestershire sauce
    1 ½ cups milk
        2 cups shredded cheddar cheese
        1 pkg. (6 to 8 oz.) brown-and-serve sausages
        1 can (any size) tiny whole potatoes
        1 pkg. English muffins
        1 pkg. (any size) cherry tomatoes

Fondue Welsh Rabbit — continued

Melt butter over low heat. Blend in flour, salt, pepper, dry mustard and Worcestershire sauce. Cook over low heat, stirring until mixture is smooth and bubbly. Remove from heat and stir in milk. Heat to boiling, stirring constantly. Boil and stir for 1 minute. Stir in cheese; heat over low heat, stirring constantly, until cheese melts. Transfer pot to warmer at the table. Adjust heat when necessary to keep fondue warm. Cut sausages into thirds and brown. Warm potatoes in sausage drippings. Cut muffins into pieces and place in oven until crisp. Arrange sausages, potatoes, muffins and tomatoes around fondue pot; dip in sauce to eat. Makes 4 servings.

Bernard Jacobson, Atchison, 1978

Beef Liver Gourmet

3 or 4 tablespoons butter or margarine
1 medium onion, chopped
1 can (6 oz.) mushrooms, drained
½ lb. beef liver, cut into 1-inch cubes
   Salt to taste
½ cup sour cream
   Toast

Melt 2 tablespoons butter in skillet over medium heat. Add chopped onion; cook until transparent. Remove onion from skillet; add mushrooms and saute. Remove mushrooms from skillet; melt remaining butter in skillet. Add liver; cook until tender. Add salt, onion, mushrooms and sour cream. Heat and stir until sauce is hot. Serve on toast. Makes 4 servings.

Janett M. Weibe, Newton, 1975

Cabbage Rolls (Microwave)

½ lb. fresh pork sausage
½ lb. ground beef
1 medium head green cabbage
2 eggs, beaten
¼ cup milk
⅓ cup quick-cooking rice
¾ teaspoon salt
¼ teaspoon pepper
¼ teaspoon mace or nutmeg
1 medium onion, finely chopped
2 cups tomato sauce

In 2-quart microwave-safe casserole or bowl, crumble pork sausage and ground beef; cook in microwave oven, uncovered, 5 minutes or until no longer pink, breaking up with a fork once. Drain. Wrap head of cabbage in waxed paper and microwave 8 minutes or until leaves are softened. Meanwhile, add all remaining ingredients except tomato sauce to meat; mix well. Remove 12 cabbage leaves (save partially cooked center and complete cooking for another meal). Place ¼ cup meat mixture on each leaf and roll to enclose meat mixture, securing with toothpicks. Place rolls, seam side down, in a 2-quart (12x7-inch) baking dish. Pour tomato sauce over rolls. Cover with waxed paper and cook 16 minutes or until cabbage is tender. Makes 12 rolls; serves 3 to 4.

Bev Careswell, Wichita, 1975

Cheese and Rye Puff

14 slices medium-size rye bread
   Soft butter or margarine
½ lb. cheddar cheese (2 cups), shredded
3 eggs
2 teaspoons grated onion
1 teaspoon dry mustard
½ teaspoon salt
   Dash of pepper
1 can (13 oz.) evaporated milk (1 ⅔ cups)
½ cup water

Butter bread slices on 1 side. Trim off and discard crusts. Cut slices into 6 pieces. Place a layer of bread slices, buttered sides up, in a 1½-quart casserole. Sprinkle layer of cheese over bread. Repeat layers until all bread and cheese are used, ending with cheese on top. In large bowl beat eggs with onion and seasonings. Add milk and water; stir to blend thoroughly. Pour mixture over bread and cheese. Let stand 30 minutes. Place casserole in larger baking pan; pour hot water around dish to a depth of about 1 inch. Bake in preheated 350-degree oven until puffy, brown and set, about 1 hour. Makes 4 to 6 servings.

Jean Kennedy, Chanute, 1981

Vegetable Casserole

1 pkg. (10 oz.) frozen chopped broccoli
⅓ cup chopped onion
1 can (6 oz.) cream-style corn
2 cups shredded cheese
3 tablespoons melted margarine
½ cup cracker crumbs
2 eggs, lightly beaten with fork
1 cup cornflake crumbs
2 tablespoons melted margarine

In microwave or pan cook broccoli and onions until almost done. In large bowl combine corn, cheese, 3 tablespoons melted margarine, cracker crumbs and eggs. Stir in broccoli and onions. Pour into a 2-quart baking dish (lightly greased). Mix cornflake crumbs with melted margarine. Sprinkle over top. Bake in 325-degree oven 1 hour. Makes 6 to 8 servings.

Mrs. Lawrence Bell, Medicine Lodge, 1982

White Lasagna

3 tablespoons butter
1 teaspoon lemon juice
1 lb. fresh mushrooms, sliced
5 tablespoons flour
½ teaspoon salt
1 teaspoon cayenne pepper
2 ½ cups milk
⅓ cup fresh minced parsley
8 oz. lasagna noodles
1 lb. cottage cheese
8 oz. mozzarella cheese
½ cup Parmesan cheese

In skillet saute 6 minutes: butter, lemon juice and fresh mushrooms. Blend in flour, salt and pepper. Gradually stir in 2½ cups milk. Cook and stir until thickened. Stir in parsley. Cook and drain lasagna noodles. Spread ½ cup mushroom sauce in 9x13-inch

White Lasagna — continued

baking dish. Make 3 layers each of the noodles, cottage cheese, mozarella, Parmesan and remaining sauce. Bake in 325-degree oven 45 minutes. Let stand 15 minutes before cutting. Makes 8 servings.

Sally J. Christensen, Winfield, 1983

Tamale Corn

1 can (15 oz.) beef hot tamales in chili sauce
1 can (16 oz.) cream-style corn
   Buttered cracker crumbs

Remove husks from hot tamales and cut tamales into 2-inch pieces. Mix tamales and their chili sauce with corn and pour into very well buttered 1-quart casserole. Top with buttered crumbs and cover. Bake in 400-degree oven until heated through, about 15 minutes. Serves 3 when used as a main dish or 6 if used as a side dish.

My twin sons are extremely fond of this and are always tickled to be served this when they come home to have lunch with me — summer or winter.

Mrs. Louis Stroop Sr., McPherson, 1986

SALADS AND VEGETABLES

Vegetables occupy more room on the plate than they did in 1955. They may, in fact, be the whole meal.

And, when temperatures soar above 100 degrees and hot winds sweep the Kansas plains, nothing's more appealing to the cook and eaters than a cold collation of salads.

The Favorite Recipe Contest has seen the number of entries for whole-meal salads increase, marveled at the growing popularity of frozen and fresh spinach and watched pasta salads outnumber potato salads.

Rice and pasta have become hot vegetable alternatives to potatoes. Introduced to cooked dry beans in Mexican and Southwestern-style foods, cooks are using them in other ways as well.

Gelatin salads, popular in the 1950s but rare in the 1970s, seem to be making a small comeback.

Contestants often note that their salad and vegetable recipes are favorites for salad suppers or carry-in dinners.

SALADS

Spinach-Brown Rice Salad

1 cup brown rice
2 cups water
½ cup bottled Italian salad dressing
1 tablespoon soy sauce
½ teaspoon sugar
2 cups fresh spinach leaves, cut into thin strips
½ cup sliced celery
½ cup sliced radishes
½ cup sliced green onions, including tops
4 strips crumbled, crisp bacon

In saucepan cook rice by bringing it and water to boil. Reduce heat and simmer 45 minutes. Transfer to serving bowl. Cool slightly. Combine dressing, soy sauce and sugar; stir into warm rice. Cover and chill. Stir in spinach, celery, radishes, green onions and bacon just before serving. Makes 6 to 8 servings.

This recipe originally called for white rice, but I wanted to add more fiber to our diet, so I tried it with brown rice and we liked it even better.

Joyce Daigh, Augusta, 1990

Jambalaya Rice Salad

2 ½ cups water
1 cup converted rice
2 teaspoons salt (divided use)
½ teaspoon hot pepper sauce
¼ cup vegetable oil
1 clove garlic, minced
½ lb. cooked shrimp or 1 to 2 cans (4 ½ oz. each)
  shrimp, drained
1 cup diced cooked ham
4 green onions, with tops, sliced
½ medium green pepper, cut in 1 ¼-inch strips
2 medium tomatoes, chopped

Bring water to boil in large saucepan. Stir in rice, 1 teaspoon salt and hot pepper sauce. Cover and simmer 20 minutes. Remove from heat. Let stand until all liquid is absorbed, about 5 minutes. Transfer rice to large bowl. Combine oil, remaining salt and garlic, mixing well. Add to rice. Stir in shrimp, ham, onions and green pepper. Chill at least 3 hours. Stir in tomatoes just before serving. Makes 6 main-course servings.

Liz Stevenson, Great Bend, 1987

Tuna-Apple Salad

1 can (6 ½ oz.) water-pack light tuna, drained
2 tablespoons grated white onion
½ cup diced celery
1 medium diced dill pickle
1 small peeled, diced apple
4 to 5 drops hot pepper sauce
2 heaping tablespoons mayonnaise

In large bowl lightly toss tuna, onion, celery, pickle and apple. In small bowl add hot sauce to mayonnaise. Add to tuna mixture and toss. Chill several hours before serving. Makes 4 servings.

Martina Muir, Harper, 1987

Irish Cucumbers

2 or 3 medium cucumbers
Sauce
   ¾ cup yogurt
   ¼ cup vinegar
   ¼ cup honey or sugar
   1 teaspoon salt
   ¾ teaspoon cracked pepper

Slice fresh cucumbers, with skins if homegrown or not waxed; pare if waxed. In medium bowl combine yogurt, vinegar, honey, salt and pepper. Stir in cucumbers. Chill. Makes 6 servings.

Margaret Kelly, Stafford, 1987

Southwest Layered Salad

   1 cup cooked pinto beans
1 ½ cups diced cooked chicken or turkey
   ¾ cup sliced celery
   ½ cup reduced-calorie mayonnaise
   ⅓ cup picante sauce
   ¾ teaspoon ground cumin
   6 cups loosely packed torn spinach
   1 cup thinly sliced red onion rings
   1 small cucumber, sliced and halved
   1 medium tomato, chopped
   1 cup coarsely crushed tortilla chips
     Picante sauce

In medium bowl combine beans, chicken or turkey and celery. In small bowl blend mayonnaise, picante sauce and cumin; add to bean mixture and mix well. Place half of spinach on bottom of 2 ½-quart clear glass bowl. Top with half the bean-meat mixture, onion rings, cucumber slices, remaining spinach and remaining bean-meat mixture. Chill. Top with tomato and chips. Toss just before serving and serve with additional picante sauce. Makes 6 servings.

Joan C. Chance, Mount Hope, 1988

Fresh Apple Salad

8 cups chopped, tart red apples (unpeeled)
1 can (20 oz.) pineapple chunks, drained (reserve juice)
2 cups seedless green grapes
2 teaspoons poppy seeds
1 ½ cups toasted pecans

Dressing

Reserved pineapple juice
¼ cup butter
¼ cup sugar
1 teaspoon lemon juice
2 tablespoons cornstarch
2 tablespoons water
½ cup reduced-calorie mayonnaise
½ cup plain yogurt

Prepare dressing first by combining reserved pineapple juice, butter, sugar and lemon juice in small saucepan. Heat to boiling. Combine cornstarch and water to make smooth paste; add to hot mixture; cook until thick and smooth, stirring constantly. Chill completely before stirring in mayonnaise and yogurt.

In large bowl combine apples, pineapple chunks, grapes and poppy seeds. Add chilled dressing and stir. Refrigerate until time to serve. Stir in pecans just before serving. Makes 16 servings.

Patty Becker, Derby, 1989

Raspberry Salad

2 pkgs. (3 oz. each) raspberry gelatin
2 ½ cups boiling water
1 ½ cups strained applesauce
    Dash of salt
1 tablespoon lemon juice
1 pkg. (10 oz.) frozen raspberries in syrup, thawed
½ pkg. (2 cups) miniature marshmallows
1 carton (8 oz.) sour cream

In large bowl dissolve gelatin in water; chill until partially set. Add applesauce, salt, lemon juice and raspberries. Chill until firm. In refrigerator container combine marshmallows and sour cream; soak in refrigerator overnight; whip and spread over gelatin mixture. Makes 8 servings.

Leota Baxter, Ingalls, 1990

Sauerkraut-Spinach Salad

1 lb. raw spinach, cleaned, stemmed and dried
1 can (16 oz.) sauerkraut, rinsed, drained and chilled
6 tablespoons sugar
2 teaspoons salt
½ cup vinegar
⅔ cup salad oil
1 medium onion, chopped very fine

In large salad bowl combine spinach and sauerkraut. In small bowl or jar mix sugar, salt, vinegar, oil and onion. Mix well and pour over spinach and sauerkraut. Toss to mix. Makes 6 to 8 servings.

M.A. Young, McPherson, 1986

Spiced Apricot Mold

1 can (16 oz.) apricot halves, drained, reserving 3/4 cup liquid
¼ cup water
1 pkg. (3 oz.) orange gelatin
2 tablespoons lemon juice
2 whole cloves
1 carton (8 oz.) plain yogurt
¼ teaspoon cinnamon
    Green grapes and parsley for garnish (optional)

Lightly oil 1-quart mold. Chop apricots; arrange evenly in bottom of prepared mold. In small saucepan combine reserved liquid and water; bring to boil. Add gelatin and lemon juice. Stir until gelatin is dissolved. Stir in cloves. Allow to stand 5 minutes. Remove cloves. Blend yogurt and cinnamon. Stir into gelatin mixture. Refrigerate until syrupy. Pour mixture over apricots in mold. Refrigerate 3 to 4 hours, until firm. To serve, unmold onto serving plate. Garnish with green grapes and parsley if desired. Makes 6 servings.

The spiced apricot salad is beautiful to the eye and delicious to the taste. It is an ideal side dish for broiled fish or meats.

Helen Nixon, Emporia, 1990

Corn Bread Salad

  1 **recipe of corn bread, using 1 ½ or 2 cups cornmeal;
      mixed, baked, cooled and crumbled**
10 **to 12 slices bacon, cooked and crumbled**
  1 **cup finely chopped celery**
  2 **fresh green onions, including tops, thinly sliced**
  2 **large tomatoes, finely chopped**
¼ **cup green pepper, finely chopped**
  2 **tablespoons chopped pimiento (optional)**
  2 **hard-cooked eggs, chopped (optional)**
      Mayonnaise

In large bowl combine crumbled corn bread, bacon, celery, onion, tomato and green pepper. Add pimiento and eggs, if desired. Add enough mayonnaise to hold together. Chill 2 or 3 hours, or overnight, before serving. Makes approximately 8 cups.

When we visit my cousin, she always has some different foods for us to try. This salad is very unusual but has an appealing taste.

Lillie Coffey, Arkansas City, 1986

Speedy Blender Gelatin

   1 **pkg. (6 oz.) strawberry flavor gelatin**
   1 **cup boiling water**
2 ½ **cups ice cubes**
   1 **carton (6 oz.) strawberry yogurt**

Combine gelatin and boiling water in blender. Blend well. Add ice cubes one at a time. Blend well. Add yogurt. Pour into gelatin mold or salad bowl. Refrigerate about 15 minutes, or until firm. Makes 4 to 6 servings.

Note: Try other flavors of gelatin and yogurt. This is a fast and easy salad to make and doesn't take many ingredients.

Rowena Hinshaw, Wichita, 1983

Artichoke Rice Salad

1 pkg. (8 or 10 oz.) chicken-flavored rice mix
4 green onions, thinly sliced
½ green pepper, chopped
12 pimiento-stuffed olives, sliced
2 jars (6 oz. each) marinated artichoke hearts
¾ teaspoon curry powder
½ cup mayonnaise

Cook rice according to package directions, omitting butter. Place rice in large bowl. Cool. Add onions, peppers and olives. Drain artichoke hearts, reserving marinade. Cut hearts in half. In small bowl combine marinade, curry powder and mayonnaise. Add artichoke hearts to rice mixture. Toss with curry dressing and chill. Makes 6 to 8 servings.

Note: To use plain rice, cook in water seasoned with chicken bouillon cube or granules. A good change from potato salad. If you add shrimp, chicken or ham, it makes a good main course.

Debi Drace, Wichita, 1985

Avocado Bean Salad

1 can (15 oz.) red kidney beans, drained
2 medium tomatoes, chopped
½ cup chopped ripe olives
1 tablespoon chopped green pepper
2 cups torn lettuce
½ cup grated cheddar cheese
½ cup lightly crushed corn chips
Dressing
1 medium avocado, mashed
½ cup sour cream
1 teaspoon minced onion
¾ teaspoon chili powder
¼ teaspoon salt
⅛ teaspoon pepper
2 tablespoons bottled Italian dressing

In small bowl combine avocado, sour cream, onion, chili powder, salt, pepper and dressing; mix well.

In salad bowl combine beans, tomatoes, olives, green pepper and lettuce; chill. Just before serving, toss with salad dressing. Sprinkle cheese and corn chips on top. Makes 6 servings.

Marie Chase, Mount Hope, 1975

Super Salad

1 head lettuce, broken and torn
4 to 8 oz. cheese, cut into squares (any kind of cheese
  may be used)
1 can (6 oz.) asparagus tips
1 can (6 oz.) baby carrots
1 apple, cut into small pieces
1 jar (4 to 6 oz.) marinated artichoke hearts
2 medium tomatoes, cut into small pieces
1 to 2 cups ham or cooked bacon
4 stalks celery, chopped
  Onion and green pepper (optional)
  Oil and vinegar to taste

In salad bowl combine lettuce, cheese, asparagus, carrots, apple, artichoke hearts, tomatoes, ham or bacon, celery and onion and green pepper, if desired. Toss to thoroughly combine. Add oil and vinegar; toss and serve. Makes 4 generous servings.

Linda Frost, Wichita, 1975

Rita's Bread Salad

1 loaf (16 oz.) sliced white bread
¼ cup finely chopped onion
5 hard-cooked eggs, diced
1 can (4 oz.) crab, drained
1 can (4 ½ oz.) shrimp, drained
1 cup diced celery
½ cup salad dressing
  Salt and pepper to taste
  Paprika

Trim crusts from bread; cut bread into cubes. In large bowl combine cubed bread, onion and eggs. Refrigerate overnight. Before serving, add crab, shrimp and celery. Fold in salad dressing and salt and pepper. Sprinkle with paprika. Makes 10 servings.

Joanne Angell, Wichita, 1978

Orange-Tuna-Macaroni Salad

½ cup mayonnaise
1 teaspoon prepared mustard
¼ teaspoon salt
⅛ teaspoon black pepper
2 large oranges, peeled and cut into bite-sized pieces
1 can (6 ½ or 7 oz.) solid tuna, drained and flaked
2 cups cooked macaroni, drained and cooled
½ cup diced celery
¼ cup finely chopped onion

In small bowl blend mayonnaise, mustard, salt and pepper. In salad bowl combine orange pieces, tuna, macaroni, celery and onion. Add mayonnaise mixture and mix lightly but thoroughly. Salad may be made ahead and refrigerated overnight. Makes 6 to 8 servings.

Mrs. Robert Bolen, Oswego, 1969

Kansas Slaw

1 medium-sized head cabbage, chopped
1 medium onion, sliced into rings
⅞ cup sugar
Dressing
1 cup vinegar
¾ cup salad oil
1 teaspoon celery seed
1 tablespoon salt
1 teaspoon dry mustard
2 teaspoons sugar

Alternate layers of cabbage and onion in large bowl; sprinkle sugar over top. In saucepan combine vinegar, oil, celery seed, salt, dry mustard and sugar; bring to boil. Pour over cabbage-onion mixture. Refrigerate about 4 hours. Stir before serving. This salad will keep up to 2 weeks in the refrigerator if kept covered. Makes 6 to 8 servings.

Mrs. W.W. Rivers, Wichita, 1971

Molded Chicken Salad

- 2 cups hot water
- 1 pkg. (3 oz.) lemon gelatin
- ¼ cup chopped green pepper
- ½ cup diced celery
- ¼ cup chopped stuffed olives
- 2 cups chopped cooked chicken
- ½ teaspoon salt
  Lettuce
  Salad dressing
  Olives

Pour hot water over gelatin and stir until dissolved; cool and chill. When gelatin is syrupy add green pepper, celery, olives, chicken and salt. Pour into ring mold which has been dipped in cold water. Chill thoroughly. Turn out onto bed of crisp lettuce. Fill center of ring with chopped lettuce and top with dressing. Decorate with slices of olives.

Mrs. Frank D. King, Augusta, 1955

Sweet Potato Salad

2 large sweet potatoes, cooked and chilled
½ cup diced celery
½ cup pineapple tidbits, drained
2 tablespoons diced green pepper
1 tablespoon honey
½ cup (approximately) sour cream
½ cup seedless red or green grapes (canned or fresh)
½ cup diced red apples
2 tablespoons diced sweet pickles
2 tablespoons diced red (sweet) pepper
1 teaspoon salt
   Pepper rings

Peel and dice sweet potatoes; put potatoes (3 cups) into large mixing bowl. Add celery, pineapple, green pepper, honey, sour cream, grapes, apples, sweet pickles, sweet pepper and salt. Toss, adding more sour cream as needed to obtain the right consistency. Heap in salad bowl and garnish with red and green pepper rings. Refrigerate until serving time. Makes 8 servings.

Mrs. M.W. McClure, Great Bend, 1961

Applesauce-Cheese Salad

⅔ cup red-hot cinnamon candies
2 pkgs. (3 oz. each) lemon gelatin
2 cups boiling water
1 ½ cups applesauce
1 pkg. (8 oz.) cream cheese
½ cup chopped nuts
½ cup finely chopped celery
½ cup mayonnaise

Place red-hots and gelatin in heat-proof bowl. Pour boiling water over them and stir until dissolved. Stir in applesauce; pour half of mixture into 8-inch pan and chill until firm; set remaining gelatin mixture aside. Soften cream cheese at room temperature; blend with nuts, celery and mayonnaise. Spread over chilled gelatin mixture. Pour on remaining gelatin and chill until firm. Makes 8 to 10 servings.

Mid Oliver and Fara Adams, Wichita, 1975

Cynthia Salad

2 cups boiling water
1 pkg. (3 oz.) lemon gelatin
1 pkg. (3 oz.) lime gelatin
1 pint (2 cups) cottage cheese
1 cup mayonnaise
1 small can (5 oz.) evaporated milk
1 can (20 oz.) crushed pineapple, drained
4 teaspoons horseradish, drained
1 cup chopped pecans (optional)

In medium bowl mix boiling water with lemon and lime gelatins and stir until dissolved. Add cottage cheese, mayonnaise, evaporated milk, pineapple, horseradish and pecans. Mix thoroughly and pour into 9x11-inch glass casserole. Refrigerate until set. Makes about 10 servings.

Alice Breitweiser, Wichita, 1975

Mixed Vegetable Souffle Salad

1 cup hot water
1 pkg. (3 oz.) lemon-flavored gelatin
½ cup cold water
4 ½ teaspoons vinegar
½ cup mayonnaise
¼ teaspoon salt
Dash of pepper
⅓ cup shredded carrot
⅓ cup sliced radishes
⅓ cup diced celery
⅓ cup chopped greens (watercress, spinach, romaine, endive or escarole)
2 tablespoons diced green pepper
1 tablespoon finely chopped onion

Pour hot water over gelatin in large bowl; stir until gelatin is dissolved. Add cold water, vinegar, mayonnaise, salt and pepper. Blend with rotary beater. Pour into standard metal loaf pan. Chill in freezer until firm about 1 inch from edge of pan but still soft in center. Turn mixture into bowl and beat with rotary beater until fluffy and thick. Fold in carrot, radishes, celery, greens, green pepper and onions. Pour into 4-cup mold or individual molds. Chill in refrigerator (not freezer) until firm. Unmold to serve. Makes 4 to 6 servings.

Mrs. Forrest H. Tull, Independence, 1964

Spicy Beet Salad

  1 can (16 oz.) diced beets
  1 pkg. (3 oz.) lemon gelatin
  1 cup boiling water
  ½ teaspoon salt
  2 tablespoons vinegar
  ¾ cup beet juice
 1 ½ cups finely chopped cabbage
 1 ½ teaspoons grated horseradish

Drain beets, reserving liquid. In large bowl dissolve gelatin in boiling water. Stir in salt, vinegar and beet juice. Chill until slightly thickened. Stir in drained beets, cabbage and horseradish. Pour into 1-quart mold or glass dish and chill until firm. Makes 6 servings.

Vesta Clark, Wichita, 1969

Fluffy Cranberry Mold

  1 large pkg. (8-serving size) cherry or other red gelatin
  1 cup boiling water
  1 can (12 oz.) ginger ale (may be dietetic)
  1 can (6 oz.) frozen orange juice concentrate (undiluted)
  1 pkg. (10 oz.) frozen strawberries, thawed and pureed in blender or food processor
  1 can (16 oz.) whole-cranberry sauce
  1 pint whipped topping

In large bowl dissolve gelatin in boiling water. Add ginger ale, concentrate and strawberries. Chill until thick. Fold in cranberry sauce and topping. Oil bundt pan or other large mold. Pour in mixture and chill. Makes approximately 16 servings.

Mari Alice Christensen, Great Bend, 1974

DRESSINGS

Pelican Honey Dressing

10 oz. mayonnaise
½ cup vegetable oil
¼ cup honey
¼ cup mustard
1 small onion, finely chopped
1 teaspoon finely chopped parsley
2 tablespoons lemon juice
1 hard-cooked egg, finely chopped
½ teaspoon salt
½ teaspoon monosodium glutamate (optional)

In large wooden bowl use wooden spoon to combine mayonnaise, oil, honey, mustard, onion, parsley and lemon juice. Stir in egg, salt and flavor enhancer, if desired. Serve with green salads of all kinds and as a cold sauce with cold chicken. This dressing will keep up to seven days in covered glass container in refrigerator. Makes about 2 cups.

Mrs. Harry Young, Andover, 1975

Pecan-Garlic Dressing

3 large garlic cloves
¼ cup coarsely chopped pecans
½ teaspoon salt
¼ teaspoon freshly ground pepper
½ teaspoon sugar
¼ cup red wine vinegar
¾ cup olive oil

In a food processor fitted with steel blade and with motor running, drop garlic through feed tube to mince. Add pecans, salt, pepper and sugar. Stop machine; scrape side of bowl. Add vinegar; process until blended, turning on and off 3 or 4 times. With motor running, add olive oil through feed tube in slow, steady stream. Process until combined. Toss dressing with favorite combination of greens. Makes about 1 cup.

Judy Juhnke, Hutchinson, 1989

Mustard-Dill Dressing Superb

1 jar (8 oz.) dijon mustard
8 oz. cider vinegar
1 tablespoon tarragon vinegar
1 tablespoon dill weed
1 quart safflower or sunflower oil
¼ cup Parmesan cheese
¼ cup light cream
1 clove garlic, minced

In medium bowl mix mustard, vinegars and dill; let stand 10 minutes. Slowly whisk in oil being poured in a constant stream so mixture is emulsified. Add cheese, cream and garlic. Refrigerate. Makes 1 ½ quarts.
This is delicious on a fresh green tossed salad.

Mrs. A.R. Markley, Plainville, 1986

London Embassy Dressing

¾ **cup sugar**
1 **cup corn oil**
½ **cup cider vinegar**
¾ **cup ketchup**
2 **teaspoons paprika**
2 **teaspoons steak sauce**
2 **small onions, grated**
2 **teaspoons salt**

In 1-quart jar mix sugar, corn oil, vinegar, ketchup, paprika, steak sauce, onion and salt; cover and shake well. Keep refrigerated. Makes 1 quart.

Note: I like this recipe as it is very simple to mix right in the quart jar. It's very tasty and a real money-saver, too. Use A-1 steak sauce.

Dorothy F. Anderes, Coffeyville, 1985

VEGETABLES

Broccoli Casserole

> 2 pkgs. (10 oz. each) chopped frozen broccoli
> 1 can (10 ¾ oz.) cream of mushroom soup
> ½ cup mayonnaise
> 2 beaten eggs
> ¾ lb. grated cheddar cheese
> 2 tablespoons dehydrated onion or ½ fresh onion, minced
> Salt and pepper to taste
> 1 teaspoon monosodium glutamate (optional)
> ½ cup crushed cheese crackers

In saucepan or microwave cook broccoli until tender. Drain well. In large bowl mix with soup, mayonnaise, eggs, cheese, onion, salt, pepper and MSG if desired. Pour into 9x13-inch baking dish. Sprinkle with crushed crackers. Bake in 350-degree oven 30 to 40 minutes. Makes 6 servings.

Linda Dale, Wichita, 1986

Muffin Mix Corn

> 1 cup sour cream
> 1 stick (½ cup) margarine
> ¼ cup chopped onion
> 1 can (17 oz.) whole kernel corn, with liquid
> 1 can (17 oz.) cream-style corn
> 3 eggs, well-beaten
> 1 pkg. (8 ½ oz.) corn muffin mix
> 1 cup grated cheddar cheese

Bring sour cream to room temperature. In skillet melt margarine and saute onion. Set aside. In large bowl mix both cans of corn with eggs. Add muffin mix and sauteed onion. Pour into greased 9x13-inch pan. Drop sour cream by spoonfuls over mixture and sprinkle with grated cheese. Bake 45 minutes at 350 degrees. Makes 12 to 15 servings.

Mary Beth Friesen, Hutchinson, 1987

Spaghetti Squash Monterey

1 **spaghetti squash**
1 **large onion, chopped**
¼ **cup butter**
2 **cups Monterey Jack cheese, shredded**
½ **cup sour cream**
¼ **teaspoon salt**
⅛ **teaspoon pepper**
  Sprinkle of paprika

Cut squash in half lengthwise and remove seeds. Place cut side down in a pot with 2 inches of water. Cover and boil 20 minutes. (Or cook squash in microwave.) After cooking, remove squash strands from shell with a fork into large bowl and discard shell. In skillet saute onion in butter until transparent. Shred cheese and divide in half. To the squash add onion, sour cream, salt, pepper and 1 cup of cheese. Place in a buttered 8x12-inch casserole and sprinkle with remaining cheese. Sprinkle paprika lightly over the top. Bake in 325-degree oven 30 minutes. Makes 6 to 8 servings.

Geneva Basore, Bentley, 1987

Hominy Casserole

2 cans (14 oz. each) yellow hominy
1 medium onion, finely chopped
3 cups shredded cheddar cheese
1 can (4 oz.) diced green chilies

Drain hominy. Put half in buttered 9x9- or 7x11-inch casserole. Sprinkle with half of the cheese and onion. Top with half the chilies. Repeat with remaining ingredients. Cover and bake 20 minutes in 400-degree oven. Makes 10 servings.

Dorothy Frey, Fredonia, 1988

Easy Baked Beans

1 large can (30 oz.) pork and beans
1 can (16 oz.) whole cranberry sauce
½ cup brown sugar, packed
¼ cup ketchup or barbecue sauce
⅛ teaspoon ginger

Put pork and beans into 2-quart baking dish. If beans are juicy, drain off some liquid and discard. Add sauce, sugar, ketchup and ginger. Mix well and bake uncovered 30 to 45 minutes in pre-heated 350-degree oven. Makes 6 to 8 servings.

This recipe is quick, easy and good hot, but we also like them cold.

Dene Smithhart, Newton, 1988

Double Good Macaroni and Cheese

8 oz. large elbow macaroni
1 lb. large-curd cottage cheese
2 cups shredded Colby cheese (divided use)
¾ cup sour cream
1 egg, beaten
2 teaspoons grated onion
1 teaspoon salt
1 teaspoon pepper

Cook macaroni; drain and set aside. In large bowl combine cottage cheese, 1½ cups Colby cheese, sour cream, egg, onion, salt and pepper. Fold in macaroni. Place in 2-quart casserole. Top with remaining ½ cup cheese. Bake uncovered in 350-degree oven until bubbly. Makes 6 servings.

Christine Hamman, Wichita, 1989

Microwave Spicy Spinach

1 box (10 oz.) frozen chopped spinach
2 cups frozen corn
1 cup jalapeno pepper cheese, diced
2 tablespoons margarine
1 tablespoon milk
Salt and pepper to taste

Remove wrapper from frozen spinach box and place box on paper towel in microwave and cook on high 5 minutes. Remove from microwave and carefully open hot box and place contents in a drainer. Cook 2 cups frozen corn in 1-quart microwave bowl for 2 minutes. While corn is cooking, squeeze water out of spinach in drainer until it is dry. Add to drained corn with cheese, margarine, milk, salt and pepper. Cook on high 2 minutes. Stir well and cook another minute. Makes 4 servings as a side dish.

Charlene Lawson, Kiowa, 1990

Vegetable Spaghetti

1 pkg. spaghetti dinner (boxed)
1 ½ cups zucchini chunks
½ cup onion, chopped
1 cup celery, sliced
1 cup carrots, thinly sliced
1 cup fresh mushrooms, sliced
3 tablespoons margarine
16 oz. cottage cheese
2 cups shredded mozzarella cheese

Prepare spaghetti dinner as directed on package. In large skillet saute zucchini, onions, celery, carrots and mushrooms in margarine. In buttered 9x13-inch pan layer half of spaghetti, sauce from spaghetti dinner, cottage cheese, vegetable mixture and mozzarella cheese. Repeat layers and sprinkle with Parmesan cheese from spaghetti dinner. Bake in 350-degree oven 30 minutes. Let stand 10 minutes before serving. Makes 6 to 8 servings.

Lori Devaney, Wichita, 1989

Savannah Red Rice

¼ lb. bacon, cooked crisp, drained and crumbled
½ cup chopped onion
½ cup chopped green pepper
¼ cup chopped celery
1 cup raw rice
1 can (16 oz.) tomatoes, pureed
1 tablespoon sugar
1 teaspoon salt
1 tablespoon chili powder
1 tablespoon liquid hot pepper sauce
1 can (16 oz.) ranch-style beans

In skillet saute onion, pepper and celery in small amount of bacon drippings. Add rice, tomatoes, sugar, salt, chili powder and hot pepper. Simmer 10 minutes. Add beans and pour into greased casserole. Sprinkle bacon on top, cover and bake in 350-degree oven 1 hour. Makes 8 to 10 servings.

Doris Phillips, Wichita, 1989

Square Lake Rice

3 strips bacon cut into small pieces
1 chopped onion
½ stick margarine or butter
1 ¼ cups uncooked white long-grain rice
1 tablespoon soy sauce
1 pkg. (2 oz.) slivered almonds
1 can (4 oz.) mushrooms
1 can (10 ½ oz.) beef broth
1 can (14 ½ oz.) beef consommé

Saute bacon, onion and butter (or margarine) together in a 3-quart saucepan until bacon is crisp and onion is cooked. Add rice, soy sauce, almonds, mushrooms, beef broth and beef consommé. Cover and simmer 20 minutes, or until rice is cooked and liquid is absorbed. Makes about 4 cups.

The recipe was introduced by one of my daughters-in-law while our family was camping at Square Lake in the Oregon mountains. Hence its name, Square Lake rice.

Evelyn Kessinger, Wichita, 1990

Onion Patties

¾ cup flour
2 teaspoons baking powder
1 tablespoon sugar
½ teaspoon salt
1 tablespoon cornmeal
½ cup non-fat dry milk (unreconstituted)
½ cup finely chopped onion
Water

In medium bowl mix flour, baking powder, sugar, salt, cornmeal and dry milk. Add enough water to make thick batter. Mix in onion and drop by spoonfuls onto hot, greased skillet or griddle. Flatten patties slightly as you turn them. Fry to golden brown. Makes about 4 servings.

These taste much like onion rings but are much easier to make.

Pat Walters, Paola, 1986

Mushroom Crust Quiche

½ lb. mushrooms
5 tablespoons butter
½ cup saltine cracker crumbs
1 bunch green onions, chopped
2 cups Monterey Jack cheese
1 cup cottage cheese
3 eggs
¼ teaspoon cayenne pepper
Paprika

Coarsely chop mushrooms and saute in 3 tablespoons butter in skillet. Mix cracker crumbs with mushrooms. Press mixture in pie pan or quiche pan. In skillet saute chopped onions in 2 tablespoons butter. Sprinkle over crust mixture. Grate cheese. In bowl mix cheese, cottage cheese, eggs and cayenne. Pour into crust. Sprinkle with paprika. Bake in 350-degree oven 40 minutes, or until knife comes out clean. Let set for 10 minutes. Makes 6 to 8 servings.

Ellen Sullivan, Valley Center, 1987

Almond Celery Bake (Microwave)

1 teaspoon margarine
1 bunch celery, chopped in food processor
½ cup slivered almonds
½ cup sharp cheese, grated
2 cans (10 ½ oz. each) cream of celery soup
1 teaspoon salt
Dash of pepper
½ teaspoon paprika
⅓ cup margarine
½ cup crushed cornflakes cereal

Grease a 9x12-inch microwave-safe baking dish with 1 teaspoon margarine. Place chopped celery in dish. Cover with almonds, then grated cheese. In small bowl combine unreconstituted soup, salt, pepper and paprika. Pour over celery layers. In microwave-safe bowl melt margarine; add cereal and mix. Sprinkle buttered crumbs on top of casserole. Microwave 12 minutes. Makes 8 servings.

Robin Ann Fiske, Wichita, 1985

Corn Curry

3 tablespoons butter or margarine
2 tablespoons chopped onion
2 tablespoons chopped green pepper
¼ to ½ teaspoon curry powder
½ cup dairy sour cream
1½ to 2 cups (1 16-oz. can) whole kernel corn
Salt and pepper to taste

Melt butter in 8-inch skillet. Add onion, green pepper and curry powder. Cover; cook over low heat till vegetables are just tender, 8 to 10 minutes. Stir in sour cream; add corn; season to taste. Heat, but do not boil, stirring constantly. Makes 4 servings.

Pat Taylor, Wichita, 1983

Celery au Gratin

2 cups sliced celery
2 tablesppons butter
2 tablespoons flour
1 cup chicken stock
¼ cup light cream
Salt and pepper to taste
¼ cup blanched almond pieces
1 cup grated cheddar cheese
¾ cup bread crumbs
2 tablespoons butter (melted)

In saucepan parboil the celery until tender. In large saucepan combine butter and flour; cook 2 minutes, then stir in chicken stock, cream, salt and pepper; cook until thick. Add celery and chopped almonds. Pour into oiled 1 ½-quart casserole. Spread cheese on top of mixture. Mix the bread crumbs and melted butter and put on top of cheese. Bake in preheated 350-degree oven 25 to 30 minutes or until brown. Makes 4 servings.

Lois Liggett, Belle Plaine, 1982

Swiss Green Beans

2 pkgs. (10 oz. each) frozen French-style green beans
Salted water
½ cup butter or margarine
1 tablespoon minced onion
⅓ cup flour
½ teaspoon dry mustard
1 teaspoon salt
¼ teaspoon pepper
2 cups milk
¾ lb. Swiss cheese, cubed
¼ cup coarsely chopped cashew nuts

Cook the green beans in boiling salted water until just tender; drain. In skillet or saucepan melt butter over low heat. Add onion and brown lightly. Stir in flour, dry mustard, salt and pepper. Gradually add milk and cook, stirring occasionally, until sauce is

Swiss Green Beans — continued

smooth and thickened. Add cheese and stir until it has melted. Combine sauce and green beans and pour into 1 ½-quart greased casserole. Sprinkle nuts over the top and bake in 350-degree oven 20 to 25 minutes. Makes 6 to 8 servings.

Mrs. Mel Sellens, Wichita, 1963

Green Bean Casserole

3   cans (15 oz. each) French-style green beans or 4 boxes (10 oz. each) frozen French-style green beans, thawed and drained but not cooked
1   can (8 oz.) water chestnuts, sliced or chopped
1   can (17 oz.) bean sprouts, drained
1   can (4 to 6 oz.) mushrooms
1   can (10 3/4 oz.) mushroom soup
½   soup can milk
¼   teaspoon dill seed (optional)
1   can french-fried onions (optional)

In large bowl combine beans, water chestnuts, bean sprouts, mushrooms, mushroom soup, milk and dill seed, if desired. Pour into oiled 9x13-inch casserole. Bake 45 minutes in 350-degree oven. Sprinkle french-fried onions over top and continue baking 15 minutes. Makes 10 to 12 servings.

Mrs. Ben Burry, Coldwater, 1960

Unbaked Baked Beans

1 can (20 oz.) pork and beans
1 small onion, finely chopped
2 tablespoons brown sugar
2 teaspoons lemon juice
½ teaspoon Worcestershire sauce
½ teaspoon paprika
¼ cup ketchup or tomato sauce
½ teaspoon liquid smoke
1 teaspoon mustard

In large skillet combine beans, onion, brown sugar, lemon juice, Worcestershire, paprika, ketchup, liquid smoke and mustard. Cover with aluminum foil and place over hot charcoal briquettes. Simmer 45 minutes. Serve with grilled hamburgers or steaks. Makes 6 servings.

Mrs. Patricia Langworthy, Derby, 1964

Scalloped Cabbage, Macaroni and Cheese

1 ½ cups macaroni
    Salted water
3 tablespoons flour
3 tablespoons butter or margarine
2 cups milk
1 teaspoon salt
2 cups shredded cabbage
½ lb. American cheese, cut in small pieces
1 cup buttered bread crumbs

Cook macaroni in boiling salted water 20 minutes; drain. In saucepan combine flour and butter; cook 2 or 3 minutes. Gradually add milk; cook and stir until thickened. Add salt. In 9x13-inch buttered baking dish, layer the macaroni, cabbage and cheese. Pour sauce over all and top with buttered bread crumbs. Bake 45 minutes in 350-degree oven. Makes 10 to 12 servings.

Mrs. Bernice Berkeybile, Ellsworth, 1975

Cabbage Chop Suey

2 tablespoons butter
1 tablespoon meat drippings or oil
4 cups shredded cabbage
1 cup diced celery
1 green pepper, minced
1 medium onion, chopped
   Salt and pepper to taste

Melt butter and drippings or oil in iron skillet or aluminum chicken fryer. Add cabbage, celery, green pepper and onion; season with salt and pepper. Cover with tight lid and steam until tender, stirring occasionally. Makes 4 to 6 servings.

Mrs. William Meng, Murdock, 1955

Spinach Casserole

2 pkgs. (10 oz. each) frozen chopped spinach
1 envelope dry onion soup
½ cup sour cream
   Buttered bread crumbs

Cook spinach according to directions on package. Drain well. In large bowl mix spinach, dry onion soup and sour cream. Place in oiled 2-quart casserole and cover with buttered crumbs. Bake 20 minutes in 375-degree oven. Makes 6 servings.

Note: If desired, completely thawed and drained chopped spinach may be used without cooking. Cornflakes, potato chips or buttered cracker crumbs may be substituted for bread crumbs.

Mrs. Darrel Hoobler, Plains, 1973

Confetti Cauliflower (Microwave)

1 medium head cauliflower
1 can (5 oz.) sliced mushrooms (do not drain)
1 can (4 oz.) chopped green chilies
1 tablespoon chopped pimientos
1 small onion, chopped
½ teaspoon seasoned pepper
½ teaspoon salt
¼ teaspoon garlic salt
½ cup grated cheddar cheese
½ cup grated mozzarella cheese

Separate cauliflower into flowerets and place in oiled, 2-quart, microwave-safe casserole. Pour mushrooms over cauliflower. Distribute green chilies, pimientos and onion over mushrooms and cauliflower. Sprinkle seasoned pepper, salt and garlic salt over cauliflower. Cover; microwave 9 minutes, stirring halfway through cooking time. At the end of cooking time, remove lid and sprinkle both cheeses over top. Return to microwave and cook 1 ½ minutes or until cheese is melted on top. Remove from oven and cover. Allow to stand for 3 minutes before serving. Makes 6 to 8 servings.

Sue Lowder, Wichita, 1975

Scalloped Beets

2 tablespoons butter
2 tablespoons flour
1 cup beet juice
2 tablespoons brown sugar
1 ½ teaspoons horseradish
12 medium beets, cooked, peeled and diced or sliced
½ cup buttered bread crumbs

Mix butter and flour in saucepan. Add beet juice and cook until thickened. Add brown sugar and horseradish. Put cooked beets in 10x11-inch baking dish. Pour cooked mixture over beets and sprinkle with bread crumbs. Bake 20 minutes in 325-degree oven, or until crumbs are browned. Makes 8 to 10 servings.

Mrs. Julian Lauterbach, Clearwater, 1978

Beets in Orange Sauce

1 tablespoon butter
1 tablespoon flour
½ cup orange juice
1 ½ tablespoons sugar
4 cups cooked beets

Melt butter in saucepan. Add flour and blend. Add juice and sugar and cook until smooth. Pour over hot beets. Let flavors blend a few minutes before serving. Makes about 6 servings.

Mrs. Frank Bestvater, Canton, 1958

Sour Cream Baked Tomatoes

5 medium tomatoes
  Salt
½ cup sour cream
⅓ cup mayonnaise
¼ teaspoon nutmeg
⅛ teaspoon dried dill seed or rosemary

Peel and core tomatoes and cut in half crosswise. Arrange in lightly oiled shallow baking dish. Sprinkle lightly with salt. In small bowl combine sour cream, mayonnaise, nutmeg and dill seed. Spread on cut surfaces of tomatoes. Bake 20 minutes in 375-degree oven until tender. Makes 6 servings.

Mrs. Sally Millikin, Fort Riley, 1968

Rosemary Parsnip Casserole

12 parsnips (about 2 lbs.)
Salted water
2 tablespoons butter
¼ teaspoon fresh or dried rosemary
2 tablespoons flour
¼ cup grated Parmesan cheese
2 cups light cream
½ cup salted round cracker crumbs mixed with ¼ cup melted butter

Peel parsnips. Cook in boiling salted water until crisp-tender. Drain and cut each half lengthwise (or slice into rounds if parsnips are large). Arrange half of parsnips in bottom of greased baking dish. Dot with butter, sprinkle with half the rosemary, flour and Parmesan cheese. Drizzle with half the cream. Repeat layers. Sprinkle buttered cracker crumbs over top of casserole. Bake uncovered in 400-degree oven 20 minutes, or until parsnips are tender. Makes 6 servings.

Mrs. Willis E. Bell, Wichita, 1976

Gourmet Potatoes

6 medium potatoes
2 cups shredded cheddar cheese
¼ cup butter
1 ½ cups sour cream
½ cup chopped onion
½ cup chopped green pepper
½ cup red pimiento
1 teaspoon salt
¼ teaspoon pepper
¼ teaspoon paprika (optional)

Cook potatoes in skins. Cool, peel and shred coarsely. In large pot over low heat combine cheese and butter. Stir until almost melted. Remove from heat and blend in sour cream, onion, green pepper, pimiento, salt, pepper and paprika. Gently stir in pota-

Gourmet Potatoes — continued

toes. Turn into buttered 9x13-inch dish, cover and refrigerate overnight. Bake next day in 350-degree oven 30 minutes. Makes 12 to 15 servings.

Kent Lawrence, Nashville, 1975

Scalloped Potatoes With Bacon and Onion

6 slices bacon
1 small onion
4 cups thinly sliced potatoes
1 teaspoon salt
1 tablespoon butter
1 tablespoon flour
⅛ teaspoon pepper
2 cups milk

Line an ungreased casserole with 3 slices of bacon. Put onion (peeled but not sliced) in center of casserole. Add half the potatoes. Season with ½ teaspoon salt. Dot with half the butter, flour and dash of pepper, rubbed together. Add rest of potatoes. Season with rest of butter, salt and pepper. Pour milk over all this. Bake 1 ½ hours uncovered in 375-degree oven. (Do not preheat oven.) Last 15 minutes of baking time, top with 3 remaining slices of bacon and continue baking. Makes 4 to 6 servings.

Mrs. Gilbert B.
Brown, Arkansas
City, 1957

Pumpkin Perfect

1 carrot
1 small onion
2 cups canned pumpkin or fresh cooked pumpkin,
drained and mashed
1 cup sour cream
1 can (10 ¾ oz.) cream of chicken soup
Salt and pepper to taste
1 pkg. (8 oz.) herb seasoned crumbs
¼ cup butter

Grate carrot and finely chop onion. In large mixing bowl combine pumpkin, sour cream and soup until blended; add carrot, onion, salt and pepper. Sprinkle half of crumbs in oiled 9x13-inch baking dish. Spoon pumpkin mixture over crumbs and top with remaining crumbs. Dot generously with butter. Bake in 350-degree oven 30 to 45 minutes. Makes 8 to 10 servings.

Karen G. Love, Wichita, 1978

Hominy Grits

¾ cup regular hominy grits
3 cups boiling water (no salt)
½ lb. sharp cheese, grated
¾ stick butter
2 eggs, well beaten
1 teaspoon salt
3 drops hot sauce
Paprika

In large saucepan add hominy grits slowly to boiling water. Cook approximately 5 minutes. Stir cheese and butter into cooked grits. Let cool. Fold in eggs. Add salt and hot sauce. Pour into 1-quart baking dish and sprinkle with paprika. Store in refrigerator overnight. Bake 1 ½ hours in 350-degree oven. Makes 8 servings.

Lois Smith, Wichita, 1978

Dairy Dream Macaroni Casserole

2 eggs, beaten
1 cup diced cheddar cheese
1 cup shredded sharp cheese
2 cups cooked macaroni
1 cup commercial sour cream
1 cup whipping cream, whipped lightly to soft peaks
4 tablespoons soft butter
1 cup toasted buttered bread crumbs

In large mixing bowl combine eggs, cheeses, macaroni, sour cream, whipped cream and soft butter. Pour into a 1 ½-quart greased casserole. Sprinkle top with crumbs. Bake in 235-degree oven 40 minutes. Makes 6 to 8 servings.

Mrs. Charles Walker, Wichita, 1964

BREADS

The most famous mistake in the history of the Favorite Recipe Contest was made in the grand-prize recipe for 1968 — garlic Parmesan loaf. Instead of 1/8 teaspoon of cayenne, the ingredients list called for 1/8 cup of cayenne. The amount is correct in the recipe in this chapter, but with the popularity of hot pepper flavor, some brave cooks may want to try increasing the amount of cayenne — just a bit.

Yeast and quick bread recipes do become treasured favorites to share. Many of them are submitted year after year, each time by a different cook.

The number of yeast bread entries declines each year. Those who do bake are putting more whole grains into their loaves.

Fruit loaves, like banana, pumpkin and zucchini breads, are standbys in Kansas kitchens. The muffin mania that began in the 1970s continues.

QUICK BREADS

Jeweled Banana Bread

1 ¾ cups flour
2 ¾ teaspoons baking powder
½ teaspoon salt
1 cup chopped walnuts
⅓ cup butter or shortening
⅔ cup sugar
2 eggs
1 cup mashed bananas
¼ cup raisins
1 cup mixed candied fruits and peels

In medium bowl stir together flour, baking powder, salt and nuts. In large bowl cream shortening and sugar until light. Add eggs one at a time and beat until thick and lemon-colored. Add flour mixture and bananas alternately, blending after each addition; fold in raisins and fruits. Grease 8½x3½-inch loaf pan on bottom, but not on sides. Pour in batter. Bake in 350-degree oven 60 to 70 minutes or until done. Let bread cool in pan 20 minutes before turning out on rack. Cool thoroughly before wrapping in foil, waxed paper or plastic wrap for storage. Makes 1 loaf.

Leota Baxter, Ingalls, 1990

Fat-Free Banana Bread

⅔ cup honey
4 egg whites
2 small ripe bananas, mashed
¼ cup non-fat yogurt
½ cup non-fat milk
¼ cup evaporated skim milk
½ teaspoon cinnamon
2 ¼ cups whole-wheat flour
1 teaspoon baking powder
1 tablespoon baking soda
½ cup raisins

In large bowl whisk together honey, egg whites, bananas, yogurt, milk, evaporated milk and cinnamon. In small bowl stir together flour, baking powder and soda, and add all at once to liquids, whisking just until blended. Do not overmix. Stir in raisins. Spread batter evenly in 13x9-inch non-stick baking pan. Bake in 350-degree oven 25 to 30 minutes or until cake tester comes out clean and bread is golden brown. Cut into squares and serve warm. Makes 10 to 12 servings.

Teresa Neal, Wichita, 1990

Pecan Corn Muffins

½ cup flaked coconut
¼ cup pecans, chopped
1 pkg. (8 ½ oz.) corn muffin mix
½ cup milk
1 egg

Preheat oven to 400 degrees. Line 12 muffin pan cups with cupcake liners. Spread coconut and pecans in jelly roll pan; bake 5 minutes or until very lightly toasted, stirring often. In medium bowl combine corn muffin mix, pecans and coconut; stir in milk and egg until just moist. Spoon batter into muffin-pan cups. Bake 20 minutes. Makes 12 muffins.

Denise Worley, Conway Springs, 1988

Morning Glory Muffins

1 ¼ cups granulated sugar
2 cups all-purpose flour
2 teaspoons cinnamon
2 teaspoons baking soda
½ teaspoon salt
½ cup coconut, shredded
½ cup raisins
2 cups shredded carrots
1 cup unpeeled, shredded apple
½ cup pecans, chopped
3 eggs
1 cup vegetable oil
½ teaspoon vanilla

Sift dry ingredients into large bowl. Add coconut, fruit, carrots and nuts; stir well. Add eggs, oil and vanilla, stirring only until combined. Spoon batter into greased muffin tins. Bake at 375 degrees for 20 minutes. Muffins are better after they ripen 24 to 48 hours. Makes 16 to 20 muffins.

This recipe was clipped from a farm paper and used many times. We like these mostly for breakfast, but they may be served as a dinner muffin. I like to warm them in the microwave, but they are good cold, too.

Mrs. Robert Jandera, Hanover, 1987

Bonanza Bread

1 cup sifted all-purpose flour
1 cup whole-wheat flour
½ teaspoon salt
½ teaspoon baking soda
2 teaspoons baking powder
⅔ cup dry non-fat milk
⅓ cup wheat germ
½ cup brown sugar
¾ cup walnuts, chopped
½ cup raisins
3 eggs
½ cup vegetable oil
½ cup light molasses
¾ cup orange juice
2 medium bananas, mashed (about 1 cup)
⅓ cup chopped dried apricots

In large bowl combine flours, salt, soda, baking powder, dry milk, wheat germ, sugar, nuts and raisins. Blend thoroughly with pastry blender or fork. Process eggs in container of electric blender or food processor until foamy. Add oil, molasses, orange juice and bananas, processing after each. Add apricots; pulse to chop coarsely. Pour mixture into bowl with dry ingredients. Stir until all flour is moistened. Pour into two 5x9-inch loaf pans. Bake 1 hour in 325-degree oven.

Note: Use any kind of nuts desired. Instead of bananas, use raw chopped apples, grated carrot, fresh ground peaches or pears, or grated zucchini. This bread is not only nutritious but tastes good, too, especially if you stick two thin slices together with cream cheese. It also freezes well.

Pat Habiger, Spearville, 1988

Pineapple Oatmeal Muffins

1 cup quick-cooking oats
1 can (8 oz.) crushed pineapple, juice pack, undrained
½ cup milk
1 egg, beaten
¼ cup butter-flavored vegetable shortening, melted
1 cup all-purpose flour
½ cup sugar
⅓ cup chopped pecans
1 tablespoon baking powder
¼ teaspoon salt
Streusel Topping
¼ cup brown sugar, firmly packed
¼ cup quick oats
¼ cup flaked coconut
¼ cup finely chopped pecans
2 tablespoons melted margarine

In small bowl mix streusel topping ingredients until crumbly. Preheat oven to 400 degrees. Grease muffin pans well; set aside. In small bowl mix oats, pineapple, juice, milk and egg. Let stand 3 minutes to soften oats. Stir in melted shortening. In medium bowl combine flour, sugar, pecans, baking powder and salt. Make well in center of mixture. Add oat mixture. Stir only until dry ingredients are moistened. Fill muffin cups about ⅔ full. Sprinkle 2 teaspoons streusel topping on top of each muffin. Bake in 400-degree oven 20 to 25 minutes, or until deep golden brown. Makes 16 muffins.

Dorothy Ann Kralicek, Wichita, 1989

Vermont Apple-Raisin Bread

1 ½ cups all-purpose flour
1 cup sugar
2 tablespoons cocoa
1 teaspoon baking soda
½ teaspoon salt
½ teaspoon cinnamon
½ teaspoon nutmeg
½ teaspoon allspice
½ cup buttermilk
1 cup applesauce
6 tablespoons melted butter or margarine
1 cup raisins
½ cup chopped walnuts

In large bowl blend flour, sugar, cocoa, baking soda, salt, cinnamon, nutmeg and allspice. In large measuring cup stir together buttermilk, applesauce and melted butter. Combine liquid and dry ingredients, stirring just until moistened. Fold in raisins and nuts. Turn into greased and floured 6½-cup tube or bundt pan. Bake in 350-degree oven 45 to 50 minutes. Cool in pan 10 minutes; then invert on rack.

Christina Wolenhaupt, Hutchinson, 1989

Broccoli Corn Bread

        1 pkg. (10 oz.) frozen chopped broccoli, thawed, drained
          and uncooked
        1 small onion, finely chopped
        2 cups cottage cheese
     1 ½ sticks margarine, melted
        5 eggs
        2 boxes (8 ½ oz. each) corn muffin mix

In large bowl thoroughly mix broccoli, onion, cottage cheese, margarine and eggs; add corn muffin mix and blend. Spread in well-greased 9x13-inch pan. Bake in 350-degree oven 45 minutes. Makes 9 to 12 servings.

Great on a fall night with a pot of ham and beans. For smaller families, cut this recipe in half. Bake in 8-inch square pan.

Kristie Jones, Wichita, 1989

Fluffy Biscuits

        6 cups biscuit mix
        1 cup tonic water
        2 tablespoons sugar
        2 tablespoons sour cream
        1 egg

In large bowl combine biscuit mix, tonic water, sugar, sour cream and egg; mix well. Roll dough about ½ inch thick and cut 15 to 20 biscuits. Preheat oven to 450 degrees. Place biscuits about 2 inches apart on well-greased cookie sheet. Bake 15 minutes. Can be frozen before baking. Need to defrost 20 minutes before baking after being frozen. Makes 15 to 20 biscuits.

Note: Tonic water is displayed in the soft drink section of the supermarket.

Anna Harrison, Liberal, 1986

Sweet and Sour Rhubarb Bread

2 ¾ cups all-purpose flour
1 ½ cups packed brown sugar
  1 teaspoon baking soda
  1 teaspoon salt
  1 egg
  1 cup buttermilk
  ½ cup vegetable oil
  1 teaspoon vanilla
  1 cup finely chopped fresh or frozen rhubarb, thawed
    and drained
  2 tablespoons all-purpose flour
  2 tablespoons butter or margarine
  2 tablespoons sugar
  ¼ cup chopped nuts

Grease four 6x3x2-inch loaf pans, three 7½x3½x2-inch loaf pans or two 8x4x2-inch loaf pans; set aside. In large mixing bowl stir together the 2¾ cups flour, brown sugar, baking soda and salt. In medium mixing bowl combine egg, buttermilk, oil and vanilla. Stir into dry ingredients, mixing well. Toss rhubarb with 2 tablespoons flour. Fold rhubarb into batter. Pour batter into prepared pans. Dot each loaf with butter and sprinkle with sugar and chopped nuts, divided evenly. Bake in 350-degree oven until wooden toothpick inserted near center comes out clean. Bake the 6x3x2-inch loaves about 40 minutes; bake the 7½x3½x2-inch loaves about 45 minutes; bake the 8x4x2-inch loaves about 55 minutes. Cool in pans 10 minutes and remove to cool on wire rack. Makes 2 to 4 loaves.

Note: This bread is especially good served warm with butter or cream cheese.

Jan Hillard, Wichita, 1985

Whole-Wheat Brown Bread

   2 **cups all-purpose flour**
  ½ **cup whole-wheat flour**
   1 **teaspoon baking powder**
   1 **teaspoon soda**
   1 **teaspoon salt**
1 ½ **cups buttermilk**
  ¼ **cup cooking oil**
  ½ **cup honey (or ¼ cup honey and ¼ cup molasses)**

In large bowl combine flours, baking powder, soda, salt, buttermilk, cooking oil and honey; mix well. Pour into greased 4½x8-inch loaf pan. Bake 40 to 50 minutes in 350-degree oven. Makes 1 loaf. (No eggs are needed in this batter.)

Joni Klaus, Wichita, 1981

Quick Anise Bread

   3 **cups all-purpose flour**
4 ½ **teaspoons baking powder**
  ½ **teaspoon salt**
  ½ **cup sugar**
   2 **eggs, beaten**
   2 **cups milk**
   2 **tablespoons butter, melted**
   5 **teaspoons anise seed**

Sift together flour, baking powder, salt and sugar. Stir in eggs and milk. Add melted butter and anise seed. Beat well and turn into 2 small (about 4½x8½-inch) well-greased loaf pans. Bake at 350 degrees for 30 minutes.

Helen Case, El Dorado, 1978

Carrot Bread

½ cup sugar
¾ cup salad oil
2 eggs, beaten
1 ½ cups grated raw carrots
1 ½ cups all-purpose flour
1 teaspoon soda
1 teaspoon salt
1 teaspoon cinnamon
½ cup chopped nuts

In large bowl cream sugar, oil and eggs. Stir in grated carrots. Sift all-purpose flour, soda, salt and cinnamon. Add to creamed mixture. Mix well. Add nuts. Bake in greased 9x5-inch loaf pan in 350-degree oven for 40 minutes. Makes 1 loaf.

Note: Delicious as sandwiches with cream cheese filling.

Alta H. Wright, Wichita, 1966

Mom's Applesauce Bread

2 cups sifted all-purpose flour
¾ cup sugar
3 teaspoons baking powder
1 teaspoon salt
½ teaspoon soda
½ teaspoon cinnamon
1 egg
1 ½ cups pink applesauce
2 tablespoons shortening, melted
½ cup nuts (optional)

Into large bowl sift all-purpose flour, sugar, baking powder, salt, soda and cinnamon. In medium bowl beat egg into applesauce. Add to dry ingredients along with melted shortening. Nuts may be added, if desired. Bake in 9x5-inch loaf pan at 350 degrees for 1 hour. Makes 8 servings.

Pat Golden, Wichita, 1964

Banana Peanut Bread

2 cups sifted all-purpose flour
1 teaspoon baking powder
½ teaspoon baking soda
½ teaspoon salt
1 egg, slightly beaten
1 cup buttermilk or sour milk
1 cup brown sugar
2 tablespoons peanut butter
1 cup mashed ripe bananas
1 cup chopped roasted peanuts

Into large bowl sift all-purpose flour, baking powder, soda and salt. In another bowl combine egg, buttermilk, brown sugar, peanut butter, bananas and chopped peanuts. Add to dry ingredients, mixing only enough to moisten. Pour into 2 greased 3½x7-inch loaf pans. Bake in 350-degree oven 1 hour. Remove to rack and cool. Makes 2 loaves.

Note: Sour milk may be made by adding 1 teaspoon vinegar to 1 cup sweet milk.

Mrs. William C. Leighnor, Goddard, 1975

Cranberry Orange Bread

    2 cups all-purpose flour
    1 cup sugar
    1 ½ teaspoons baking powder
    ½ teaspoon salt
    ½ teaspoon soda
      Grated rind of 1 orange
    1 egg, beaten
      Juice of 2 oranges
    3 tablespoons shortening, melted
      Warm water
    1 cup chopped nuts
    1 cup sliced cranberries

Into large bowl sift flour, sugar, baking powder, salt and soda. In small bowl add grated orange rind to beaten egg. Put orange juice in measuring cup and add shortening, then fill with warm water to ¾ cup. Mix with egg mixture. Add to dry ingredients. Add nuts and cranberries. Bake in greased 3x11-inch loaf pan or two 3x6-inch pans in 325-degree oven 1 hour or until done.

Mary Fry, Wichita, 1958

Raisin Bran Muffins
(Six Week Bran Muffins)

    1 box (15 oz.) Raisin Bran cereal
    5 cups sugar
    5 cups all-purpose flour
    5 teaspoons soda
    2 teaspoons salt
    4 eggs, beaten
    1 cup shortening, melted
    1 quart buttermilk

In extra-large bowl mix cereal, sugar, flour, soda and salt. Add eggs, shortening and buttermilk. Beat well. Store in covered container in refrigerator and use as desired. Fill muffin cups ⅔ full and bake in 400-degree oven 15 or 20 minutes.

Sharilyn Gump, Wichita, 1972

Graham Apple Muffins

16 graham crackers
¼ teaspoon salt
2 tablespoons sugar
½ cup milk, scalded
1 egg, beaten
2 tablespoons shortening, melted
2 teaspoons baking powder
2 cooking apples
  Cinnamon

Crush and roll crackers. Place in large mixing bowl and add salt, sugar and hot milk. Mix well. Add egg and shortening. Sift baking powder over batter and mix well. Fill greased muffin pans half full. Pare, core and slice apples. Place 2 or 3 apple slices on top of each portion of batter and sprinkle with cinnamon. Bake in 400-degree oven 20 to 25 minutes. Makes 1 dozen muffins.

Mrs. Darrel Hoobler, Plains, 1976

Fluffy Raisin Muffins

⅔ cup raisins
2 cups all-purpose flour
¼ cup sugar
1 teaspoon salt
3 teaspoons baking powder
¼ cup shortening
1 egg, beaten
1 cup buttermilk

Rinse and drain raisins. Into large bowl sift together flour, sugar, salt and baking powder. Cut shortening into flour mixture with pastry blender or fork. In small bowl combine beaten egg and buttermilk and stir into flour mixture. Stir in raisins. Fill well-greased muffin cups ¾ full. Bake in 425-degree oven 10 to 25 minutes. Makes 1 dozen.

Margaret Gegen, Colwich, 1978

Upside-Down Cranberry Muffins

3 tablespoons butter or margarine
1 ¼ cups sugar
1 ½ cups coarsely chopped fresh or frozen cranberries
2 cups sifted all-purpose flour
1 tablespoon baking powder
½ cup sugar
1 teaspoon salt
½ cup butter or margarine
1 egg
1 cup milk

In small bowl combine 3 tablespoons butter and 1¼ cups sugar. Divide equally into 12 3-inch greased muffin cups. Sprinkle cranberries into cups. Into large bowl sift together all-purpose flour, baking powder, ½ cup sugar and salt. Cut in butter to make fine crumbs. In small bowl combine egg and milk and add to flour. Stir just to mix. Batter will be slightly lumpy. Spoon into prepared muffin cups. Bake in 400-degree oven about 25 minutes. Invert onto waxed paper while warm. Makes 1 dozen large muffins.

Mrs. Ted Palsmeier, Conway Springs, 1970

Whole-Wheat Muffins

¾ cup all-purpose flour
1 cup whole-wheat flour (do not sift)
4 teaspoons baking powder
½ teaspoon salt
¼ cup sugar
1 egg
1 cup milk
¼ cup salad oil or melted shortening

Grease 16 muffin cups (about 3 inches diameter). Into medium-size mixing bowl, sift white all-purpose flour. Add unsifted whole-wheat flour, baking powder, salt and sugar. Beat egg until frothy. Add milk and salad oil. Mix well. Make a small well in flour mixture and pour in milk mixture all at once. Stir quickly and lightly, but do not beat. Quickly fill prepared muffin cups ⅓ full. Bake 35 minutes in preheated 375-degree oven. Makes about 16 muffins.

Jaine B. Brannum, Independence, 1975

Pumpkin Waffles

1 cup all-purpose flour
¾ cup whole-wheat flour
4 teaspoons baking powder
1 teaspoon salt
¾ teaspoon cinnamon
¼ teaspoon nutmeg
3 eggs
1 ¾ cups milk
½ cup oil
½ cup canned pumpkin

In large bowl stir together flours, baking powder, salt, cinnamon and nutmeg. In medium bowl beat eggs; add milk, oil and pumpkin; mix. Add to dry ingredients. Pour onto hot waffle iron and bake. Makes 4 9-inch waffles.

Paula G. Webb, Wichita, 1987

Bacon Cornmeal Waffles

   2 eggs
1 ¾ cups milk
   1 cup cake flour, or ⅞ cup all-purpose flour
2 ½ teaspoons baking powder
   1 tablespoon sugar
   ½ teaspoon salt
   1 cup yellow cornmeal
   5 tablespoons bacon fat or melted shortening
   6 to 12 slices bacon, cooked to taste

In medium bowl beat eggs slightly. Add milk. In another large bowl sift together flour, baking powder, sugar and salt. Add cornmeal. Combine liquid wilth dry ingredients and stir in melted shortening. Heat waffle iron. Place ½ strip bacon on each section and pour batter over bacon. Cook waffles until crisp. Remove excess fat from waffle iron with absorbent paper. Number of waffles depends on size of waffle iron.

Mrs. Raymond Seiler, Colwich, 1957

Pioneer Pancakes

   2 cups boiling water
1 ½ cups yellow cornmeal
   2 tablespoons dark molasses
   2 cups sour milk or buttermilk
   4 eggs
   3 cups sifted all-purpose flour
   6 teaspoons baking powder
   3 teaspoons salt
   ½ teaspoon soda
   6 tablespoons butter, melted

Pour boiling water over cornmeal in large bowl, stirring until thick and partially cooled. Stir in molasses, then milk. Add unbeaten eggs and beat in. Sift all-purpose flour with baking powder, salt and soda. Stir into batter. Add melted butter. Bake in

Pioneer Pancakes — continued

any desired size on a hot buttered griddle. For 7-inch jumbo pancakes, use ½ cup batter for each. It is best to place batter in a pitcher or large measuring utensil with a spout. Pour gently and steadily onto the center of the griddle to make pancakes round with uniform edges. Serve with heated syrup or spread with chipped beef or other dry meat. Also, can be rolled to make a main dish with or without gravy.

Mrs. Jesse Freeman, Danville, 1956

Oatmeal Pancakes

1 ¼ cups old-fashioned or quick oats
  2 cups skim milk
  1 egg
  ¼ cup wheat germ
  ¼ cup whole-wheat flour
  ¼ cup all-purpose flour
  1 tablespoon baking powder
  2 teaspoons sugar
  2 teaspoons vegetable oil
  ½ teaspoon salt
  1 cup fresh or frozen blueberries (optional)
    Syrup or fruit topping (optional)

In large bowl combine oats and milk and let stand 10 minutes. Stir in egg, wheat germ, flours, baking powder, sugar, oil and salt. Heat a non-stick pan over medium-low heat. Pour ¼ cup batter per pancake into hot pan. Sprinkle a few blueberries on top of each pancake, if desired. Cook, turning once, until golden brown on both sides. Serve with syrup or fruit topping. Makes 12 pancakes.

The recipe comes from "The T-Factor Diet" by Martin Katahn. My husband became very concerned about his fat intake a few years ago, and we found that this book has several good low-fat recipes in it. These pancakes are not as heavy and filling as regular pancakes. We added blueberries to the recipe for a little more sweetness.

Trisha Berry, Haysville, 1990

Danish Dumplings

½ **cup butter or margarine**
1 **cup milk**
1 **cup flour**
¼ **teaspoon salt**
4 **eggs**
 Meat broth

Place butter or margarine and milk in saucepan and bring to boil. Add all at once the flour and salt. Stir quickly until dough loosens from sides of pan. Remove from heat and allow to cool slightly. Add eggs one at a time and beat well after each addition. Drop by teaspoonfuls into boiling broth. Cook over low heat until dumplings float on top, about 15 minutes. Makes about 6 servings.

Mrs. Max Robertson, Marion, 1956

YEAST BREADS

Mincemeat Swirly Buns

¾ cup milk
½ cup sugar
2 teaspoons salt
½ cup (1 stick) margarine
2 pkgs. dry yeast
½ cup warm water
1 egg
4 cups unsifted all-purpose flour
1 jar (1 lb. 12 oz.) mincemeat
  Confectioners' sugar icing

In saucepan or microwave container scald milk; stir in sugar, salt and margarine. Cool to lukewarm. In large bowl dissolve yeast in warm water. Stir in lukewarm milk mixture, egg and half of the flour. Beat until smooth — may use mixer. Stir in rest of flour by hand to make stiff batter. Cover tightly with aluminum foil or plastic wrap. Refrigerate at least 2 hours or overnight. Dough may be refrigerated up to 2 days. Divide dough in half. On floured board, roll one half in 18x9-inch rectangle. Spread with half of mincemeat. From the 18-inch side, roll up as for jelly roll; seal edges. Cut into 1½-inch slices. Place in greased muffin cups, cut side up. Repeat with rest of dough and mincemeat. Cover and let rise in warm, draft-free place until doubled, for about 1 hour. Bake in a 350-degree oven about 20 minutes or until done. Frost with confectioners' sugar icing while warm. Makes 24 buns.

Louise M. Curtis, Hudson, 1986

German Coffee Cake

1 pkg. dry yeast
2 tablespoons lukewarm water
½ cup butter or margarine
½ cup sugar
3 eggs, beaten
½ cups scalded milk, cooled to lukewarm
4 cups all-purpose flour
½ teaspoon salt
1 cup raisins
  Melted butter
1 cup sugar mixed with 1 teaspoon cinnamon

In small bowl or cup dissolve yeast in water. In large bowl cream butter and sugar and add eggs. Add milk, flour, salt and dissolved yeast. Beat well; stir in raisins. Cover and let rise until light, about 1½ hours. Beat again with spoon. Pour into 3 well-greased 9-inch layer pans. Brush with butter and sprinkle with sugar-cinnamon mixture. Let rise 1½ hours. Bake in 375-degree oven 25 to 30 minutes, or until done. Makes three 9-inch coffee cakes.

Ruby Koehn, Dodge City, 1986

Apple Cinnamon Puffs

2 cups all-purpose flour
1 pkg. quick-rise yeast
2 tablespoons sugar
½ teaspoon salt
¾ cup warm water
¼ cup oil
1 egg
1 cup chopped apples
Topping
¼ cup sugar
1 teaspoon cinnamon
¼ cup finely chopped peanuts
3 tablespoons butter, melted

In large mixer bowl combine 1 cup flour, yeast, 2 tablespoons sugar and salt; mix well. Add very warm water (120 to 130 degrees) and oil to flour mixture. Add egg. Blend at low speed until moistened; beat 3 minutes at medium speed. By hand, gradually stir in apples and remaining flour to make a soft batter. Spoon into well-greased muffin pan cups. Cover; let rise in warm place until double, 30 minutes. Bake in 375-degree oven 15 to 20 minutes, until golden brown. In small bowl combine ¼ cup sugar, cinnamon and nuts. Dip tops of hot rolls into melted butter, then into sugar-cinnamon mixture. Serve warm. Makes 12 rolls.

Mrs. Paul Bauer, Wichita, 1987

Moosie's Bread

1 cup rolled wheat (or rolled oats)
2 cups boiling water
2 pkgs. dry yeast
⅓ cup lukewarm water
½ cup honey (or ½ cup molasses, or ¼ cup honey and ¼ cup orange marmalade)
2 ½ teaspoons salt
2 tablespoons softened butter
6 cups all-purpose flour

Preheat oven to 325 degrees. Place rolled wheat (or oats) in large mixing bowl; pour 2 cups boiling water over wheat and let stand approximately 30 minutes. In small bowl sprinkle yeast over lukewarm water and let stand 5 minutes. When wheat has soaked for 30 minutes, add honey, salt and softened butter. Stir. Stir yeast until it is dissolved, then stir into the rolled wheat mixture. Slowly work in 6 cups flour. On a floured surface, knead until dough is firm but not sticky. Add a bit more flour, if necessary. Place in greased bowl, cover with towel and let rise until doubled in bulk. Punch dough down and divide into 2 greased bread tins (or 1 regular bread tin and 6 miniature tins). Cover all tins of dough with cloth. Let dough rise again to desired height and bake in preheated oven approximately 50 minutes. For soft crust, coat top of each loaf lightly with the end of a stick of butter after loaves have been turned from pans onto cooling rack.

Note: Sometimes I substitute ½ cup of wheat germ for ½ cup of flour.

My own children, when growing up, used to love to carry the little loaves in their little hands and eat the bread just as it came from the oven and cooled enough for them to carry. They still tell anyone (who will listen) how wonderful my homemade bread is and how they remember looking forward to having their own little nutritious loaf! I have baked this bread using each of the substitutes mentioned in the list of ingredients . . . each way is delicious. Once you've baked this bread, you'll never be satisfied to bake bread any other way.

Beverlee Nowlin, Wichita, 1987

Pineapple Whole-Wheat Rolls

1 can (8 oz.) crushed pineapple
1 cup all-purpose flour
1 pkg. active dry yeast
⅓ cup milk
3 tablespoons brown sugar
3 tablespoons cooking oil
¼ teaspoon salt
2 to 2 ¼ cups whole-wheat flour
¼ cup honey
¼ cup melted butter

Drain pineapple, reserving ⅓ cup juice. Set pineapple aside. In large bowl combine all-purpose flour and yeast. In saucepan or microwave container heat reserved juice, milk, brown sugar, cooking oil and salt just until warm (120 degrees). Add to flour mixture; beat at low speed of mixer 30 seconds. Beat at high speed 3 minutes. Stir in pineapple. Stir in whole-wheat flour to make soft dough. Turn out onto floured surface; knead in enough remaining flour to make moderately stiff dough. Place in greased bowl. Cover; let rise in warm place until double (1 hour). Punch down; let rest 10 minutes. Divide dough into thirds. Shape each third into 15 balls. Place 3 balls in each cup of greased muffin tins. Let rise in warm place till nearly double (20 minutes). Bake in 375-degree oven 15 minutes. Combine honey and melted butter. Turn rolls out of cups; brush with honey mixture. Makes 15 rolls.

Sondra Meeds, Oakley, 1987

Graham or Whole-Wheat Rolls

1 pkg. dry yeast
¼ cup sugar
¼ cup butter or margarine
⅔ cup milk
½ teaspoon salt
2 eggs
⅔ cup whole-wheat or graham flour
1 ⅔ cups all-purpose flour
Flour for rolling surface

In small container mix yeast and sugar. In saucepan or microwave container scald butter and milk; turn into large mixing bowl. When lukewarm, stir in yeast and sugar, salt and eggs. Add flours and mix well. Cover bowl with waxed paper, then with cloth, and put in the refrigerator for 6 hours or overnight. On lightly floured surface roll with rolling pin and cut as for biscuits. Let rise about 2 hours or until double in size on a greased cookie sheet. Bake in 400-degree oven 10 minutes. Makes about 18 rolls.

This recipe could be used for cinnamon rolls or crescent rolls. These hot rolls are so light and good everyone usually eats more than one. They are quick and easy to make with no last-minute work except to put them in the oven. This recipe was given to me by a great-aunt and was dated 1943.

LaRena Goldak, Wichita, 1988

Buttermilk Yeast Buns

1 pkg. active dry yeast
¼ cup warm water (110-115 degrees)
3 cups buttermilk, at room temperature
½ cup sugar
½ cup melted butter
2 eggs
1 teaspoon baking soda
1 teaspoon salt
8 cups all-purpose flour
   Melted butter

In large mixing bowl stir yeast into warm water. Add buttermilk and sugar and let mixture stand 15 minutes. Add warm butter and eggs; mix. Sift soda and salt with 4 cups flour; add to liquid mixture. Beat until smooth batter forms. Add remaining flour, stirring with spoon until dough is no longer sticky. Knead on floured board; place in large greased mixing bowl. Cover; let rise until double. Punch down dough and form into buns the size of an egg. Place on greased baking sheet; flatten slightly with hand. Let rise until double, about 30 minutes. Bake in 400-degree oven 15 to 20 minutes, or until light brown. Remove to cooling rack; brush tops with melted butter. Makes about 4 dozen buns.

Barbara Riggs, Conway Springs, 1988

Jay's Glazed Oatmeal Raisin Bread

1 ½ cups raisins
1 ½ cups water
1 cup rolled oats
⅓ cup firmly packed brown sugar
3 teaspoons salt
3 teaspoons cinnamon
1 ½ cups boiling water
½ cup molasses
8 ½ to 9 ½ cups all-purpose flour
2 pkgs. regular or quick-rise yeast
1 cup water
½ cup milk
⅓ cup shortening
3 tablespoons melted margarine (optional)
Glaze
2 cups confectioners' sugar
3 tablespoons milk
1 teaspoon vanilla extract

In medium saucepan bring raisins and 1½ cups water to boil. Simmer 10 minutes, drain and cool. In medium bowl combine rolled oats, brown sugar, salt, cinnamon, 1½ cups boiling water and molasses. Mix well. In large mixing bowl combine 3 cups flour and yeast; blend well. In small saucepan (or may use 2-cup glass measure in microwave) heat 1 cup water, milk and shortening until very warm (120 to 130 degrees). Add this mixture and oats, brown sugar and molasses mixture to flour and yeast in large bowl. Blend at low speed with an electric mixer until moistened, about 1 minute; beat 4 minutes at medium speed, scraping bowl with spatula. With spoon, stir in cooled raisins and 5 cups flour to form stiff dough. On floured surface, knead in remaining flour until dough is smooth and elastic, about 10 minutes. Place in greased bowl, cover with towel and let rise in a warm place until light and doubled in size. Punch dough down, divide into 3 equal parts; shape into loaves. Place in 3 greased 9x5-inch loaf pans. Cover and let rise in a warm place until doubled in size. Preheat oven to 350 degrees and bake 35 to 45 minutes, until loaves sound hollow when lightly tapped. Remove from

Jay's Glazed Oatmeal Raisin Bread — continued

pans immediately when done. If desired, brush the tops with melted margarine.

In a small bowl combine confectioners' sugar, milk and vanilla; blend until smooth. Drizzle over warm loaves. Makes 3 loaves.

My brother, Jay Plank, gave me this recipe several years ago when he was a "house husband" and exploring the joys of cooking. This bread freezes well and is delicious toasted for breakfast. My loaves usually don't last very long frozen, as my children prefer this bread over "store-bought" raisin breads.

Marianne Bass, Wichita, 1989

Orange Dinner Rolls

1 ¾ **cups sugar, divided use**
¼ **cup grated orange peel**
6 **cups all-purpose flour**
¼ **teaspoon salt**
3 **pkgs. dry yeast**
½ **cup softened margarine**
1 **cup hot tap water**
3 **eggs**
½ **cup melted margarine**

In small bowl mix 1 cup sugar and grated orange peel to make a topping; set aside. In a large mixing bowl thoroughly mix 1¼ cups flour, remaining ¾ cup sugar, salt and undissolved yeast. Add softened margarine and gradually add tap water. Beat 2 minutes at medium speed. Scrape bowl; add eggs and ¼ cup flour. Beat at high speed 2 minutes; add remaining flour to make a soft dough. Turn out on floured board and knead until smooth and elastic. Divide dough into 3 equal pieces. Divide each piece into 8 equal balls. Dip each ball into melted margarine, then coat with orange peel topping. Arrange 8 balls in each of 3 greased 8-inch round baking pans. Let rise; bake in 350-degree oven 25 minutes. Remove from pans and cool on wire rack. Makes 24 rolls.

Donna McComb, Stockton, 1989

Dark Pumpernickel Bread

      3 pkgs. active dry yeast
  1 ¾ cups warm water
      ½ cup dark molasses
      2 tablespoons vegetable oil
      1 tablespoon caraway seeds
      1 tablespoon salt
  2 ½ cups dark rye flour
      1 cup whole-bran cereal
      ¼ cup cocoa
      2 to 2 ½ cups all-purpose flour
        Cornmeal
        Margarine, softened

In very large bowl, dissolve yeast in warm water. Stir in molasses, oil, caraway seeds, salt, rye flour, bran cereal and cocoa. Beat until smooth. Stir in enough all-purpose flour to make dough easy to handle. On lightly floured surface, let dough rest 15 minutes. Meanwhile, wash bowl, dry and grease. Knead dough 5 minutes, or until smooth and elastic. Place in bowl and turn dough so greased side is up. Cover and let rise in warm place until double, about 1 hour. Grease large cookie sheet and sprinkle with cornmeal. Punch dough down. Divide into 2 equal pieces. Shape each half into a ball and place at opposite corners of prepared cookie sheet. Brush tops with softened margarine. Let rise until double, 45 to 50 minutes. Heat oven to 375 degrees. Bake loaves until they sound hollow when tapped, about 35 minutes. Remove and cool. Wrap in plastic wrap to store. Makes 2 loaves.

The secret ingredient that brings out the fragrance and flavor of this German bread is cocoa. Spread a little liverwurst on this bread and is it "wunderbar."

Karen Moser, Winfield, 1990

Bran Rolls

¾ **cup all-bran cereal**
½ **cup sugar**
1 ½ **teaspoons salt**
½ **cup margarine or vegetable oil**
½ **cup boiling water**
½ **cup warm water (105-115 degrees)**
2 **pkgs. active dry yeast**
1 **egg, beaten**
3 ½ **to 3 ¾ cups all-purpose flour**
2 **tablespoons butter, melted**

In small bowl combine cereal, sugar, salt and margarine. Add boiling water and stir to melt margarine; cool. In large bowl stir warm water and yeast until yeast is dissolved. Beat in lukewarm bran mixture, beaten egg and 1½ cups flour. Beat 3 minutes at medium speed with mixer. Stir in additional flour until dough pulls away from sides of bowl. Turn dough onto floured surface. Knead until smooth and elastic, about 10 minutes. Wash and grease large bowl. Place dough in greased bowl, cover and let rise in warm place until doubled in size, about 1 hour. Grease a 13x9-inch baking pan. Punch down dough. Divide in half; form 2 balls. Cover half of dough with an inverted bowl. Divide remaining dough into 12 equal pieces. Shape each piece into a smooth ball. Place in greased pan. Repeat with second ball of dough. Brush tops with melted butter. Cover and let rise in a warm place until doubled in size, about 1 hour. Preheat oven to 375 degrees. Bake 20 to 25 minutes or until deep golden brown. Remove immediately from pan and cool on wire racks. Makes 24 rolls.

I make these rolls at holiday time and other occasions. It came from a book of state fair recipes at the Minnesota State Fair.

Barbara Mason, Kingman, 1990

Bake Shop Cinnamon Rolls

4 cups all-purpose flour (approximately)
1 pkg. dry yeast
1 ¼ cups milk
¼ cup sugar
¼ cup butter
Salt
1 large egg

Cinnamon filling

3 tablespoons sugar
3 tablespoons light brown sugar
1 rounded tablespoon cinnamon
2 tablespoons red cinnamon candies, finely chopped or crushed
1 teaspoon flour
4 tablespoons butter, melted
3 tablespoons cold butter

Glaze

1 cup confectioners' sugar
½ teaspoon vanilla
Half-and-half

In large bowl mix 1½ cups flour with yeast. Heat milk, sugar, butter and salt in small saucepan just until warm, 115 to 120 degrees. Stir constantly until butter almost melts. Add to yeast mixture; add egg. Beat at low speed of mixer 1 minute, scraping bowl. Beat 3 minutes at high speed. By hand stir in enough remaining flour to make a soft dough. Turn out onto lightly floured surface and knead until smooth and elastic, about 8 minutes. Shape into ball. Place in lightly greased bowl; turn once to grease surface. Cover; let rise in warm place until double, about 1½ to 2 hours. Punch down, turn out on floured surface. Cover; let rest 10 minutes. For filling mix sugars, cinnamon, chopped candies and flour. Brush two 9-inch cake pans with 1 tablespoon each melted butter. Roll dough on lightly floured surface to a thin rectangle that is about 12x20 inches. Brush dough generously with remaining melted butter. Sprinkle with cinnamon mixture. Slice cold butter into 12 pats. Place pats of butter at 1-inch intervals along one 12-inch side of the dough. The idea is to have a pat of butter in the center of each cinnamon roll. Roll up jelly-roll fashion,

Bake Shop Cinnamon Rolls — continued

starting at 12-inch side containing butter. You should create a fat log 12 inches long. Cut rolls at 1-inch intervals, using the following method: Place a piece of thread under the rolled dough and pull up and around sides; crisscross thread at top, then pull quickly. (Using the thread to cut the dough eliminates applying pressure with a knife, which would squash the rolls.) Put rolls, cut sides up, in buttered pans. Drizzle any remaining melted butter over all. Let rise, covered, in warm place 20 minutes. Heat oven to 375 degrees. Bake rolls until puffed and golden brown, 20 to 25 minutes. Cool in pans 10 minutes. For glaze mix sugar, vanilla and enough half-and-half to make medium-thick glaze. Remove rolls from pans and drizzle with glaze. Serve warm. Makes 12 large rolls.

These rolls are out of this world. They taste just like the rolls sold in a popular chain of cinnamon roll shops. I have never had a failure with this recipe.

Verdel Krug, La Crosse, 1990

Overnight Shredded Wheat Biscuits

1 ½ cups all-purpose flour
½ cup crushed shredded wheat biscuit cereal
2 tablespoons sugar
1 teaspoon baking powder
½ teaspoon baking soda
½ teaspoon salt
3 tablespoons margarine
1 pkg. dry yeast
¼ cup warm water (105 to 115 degrees)
⅔ cup buttermilk

In large bowl combine dry ingredients; cut in margarine. In small bowl dissolve yeast in warm water. Combine yeast and buttermilk; add to flour mixture, blending well. Cover and chill overnight. Next morning, turn dough out on floured surface and knead 1 minute. Roll to ½-inch thickness; cut with 2-inch biscuit cutter. Place on baking sheet. Bake in 425-degree oven 12 minutes. Makes about 12 biscuits. Dough may be refrigerated 3 to 4 days.

Marian Flanigan, Arkansas City, 1984

French Market Doughnuts

¼ cup warm water
1 teaspoon sugar
1 ¼ teaspoons dry yeast
½ cup milk
3 tablespoons sugar
1 ½ teaspoons salt
2 tablespoons shortening
½ cup cold water
1 egg white
½ teaspoon vanilla
2 ½ cups unsifted, unbleached flour
Shortening or oil for frying
Confectioners' sugar

Put warm water in large mixing bowl. Stir in sugar and yeast. Scald milk in saucepan or microwave container. Remove from heat and stir in sugar, salt and shortening. Add cold water and add to yeast mixture. Put in egg white, vanilla and flour and beat until smooth; cover and let stand 30 minutes. Heat deep-fat fryer to 370 degrees. Dough will be very soft — more like heavy batter. Scoop half of dough at a time onto heavily floured surface. Roll out with well-floured rolling pin to an 8x10-inch rectange. Dough will be ⅛ to ¼ inch thick. Cut with pizza cutter or sharp knife into 2½-inch squares. Fry about 3 at a time in deep fat until crisp and brown on underside. Turn once and brown other side. Remove and drain on paper towels. Sprinkle with confectioners' sugar and serve hot. An electric tray will help keep them hot. Makes 24.

Patricia Habiger, Spearville, 1985

Family Reunion Buns

⅔ cup milk
⅔ cup sugar
1 teaspoon salt
⅓ cup margarine
2 pkgs. dry yeast
⅔ cup warm water (110 degrees)
3 beaten eggs
6 ¾ cups sifted all-purpose flour, divided use
½ teaspoon nutmeg
1 to 2 tablespoons soft shortening or margarine

In saucepan or microwave container scald milk and stir in sugar, salt and margarine. Set aside and cool to lukewarm. In large bowl sprinkle yeast into warm water, stirring to dissolve. Add lukewarm milk mixture to yeast mixture. Blend well. Mix in beaten eggs, 3 cups flour and nutmeg. Beat until smooth. Stir in remaining flour and turn dough out on lightly floured board. Knead dough until smooth and elastic, about 10 minutes. Place in large, greased bowl and brush top with soft shortening. Cover and let rise in warm place, free from draft, until double in bulk, about 1 hour. Punch down and turn out onto lightly floured board. Divide dough in half. Cut each half into 12 equal parts. Using palms of hands, form each piece into a ball. Place about 2 inches apart on greased cookie sheet. Brush lightly with melted butter or margarine. Cover and let rise until double in bulk, about 1 hour. Bake in 400-degree oven 10 to 15 minutes. Makes 24 buns.

Joleen Bolinger, Olpe, 1982

Country Health Bread

6 ¼ to 6 ½ cups all-purpose flour
1 cup whole-wheat flour
2 pkgs. yeast
1 cup quick-cooking rolled oats
1 cup whole bran cereal
1 cup raisins
2 ½ cups boiling water
1 ½ cups cream-style cottage cheese (12 oz.)
2 tablespoons shortening
2 teaspoons salt
½ cup molasses

In large bowl mix 2 cups all-purpose flour, whole-wheat flour and yeast. In second bowl mix oats, bran cereal, raisins, boiling water, cottage cheese, shortening and salt. When shortening has melted, add molasses. Pour liquid mixture into dry mixture. Beat ½ minute on low speed of mixer, then 3 minutes on high speed. Add remainder of flour. Knead well. Cover and let rise in warm place until doubled in bulk. Punch down. Divide into 3 portions. Cover and let rest 10 minutes. Place in 3 greased standard loaf pans. Cover and let rise until double in bulk, about 45 minutes. Bake in 375-degree oven 35 to 40 minutes.

Susan Robertson, Wichita, 1974

Wheat Germ Bread

1 ½ **cups warm water**
¼ **cup molasses**
1 **cup wheat germ**
1 **pkg. dry yeast**
2 **teaspoons salt**
2 **egg yolks**
⅓ **cup corn oil**
1 **cup dry non-fat milk**
4 **cups all-purpose flour**

Pour warm water into large bowl. Add molasses and wheat germ. Sprinkle yeast over mixture and let stand 10 minutes. Add salt, egg yolks, oil and dry milk. Mix with fork. Gradually blend in flour. Dough will be dry and lumpy. Cover and set in warm place for 30 minutes. Blend again with fork. Cover. Let double. Turn out onto board and shape into loaves. Place in greased 8x4-inch pans. When dough rises level with pan, place in cold oven. Heat oven to 350 degrees and bake 40 to 45 minutes. Cool on racks. Makes 2 loaves.

Mrs. Cecil H. Fitzgeralds, Herrington, 1975

Blender Pop-Up Bread

1 cup hot tap water
½ cup dry non-fat milk
¼ cup salad oil
¼ cup sugar
1 teaspoon salt
2 eggs
1 pkg. dry yeast
3 ¼ cups all-purpose flour

In large bowl combine water, dry milk, oil, sugar, salt, eggs and yeast; blend 2 or 3 minutes. Stir in flour. Let rise 1½ hours. Grease two 1-pound coffee cans and divide dough between them. Put lids on and allow to rise until lids pop off cans. Bake in 375-degree oven 35 minutes. Allow to cool in cans for 15 minutes. Remove and cool on racks.

Mrs. Hugh J. Woods, Smith Center, 1975

Swedish Raisin Rye Bread

2 cups raisins
Water
3 cakes compressed yeast (or 3 pkgs. dry yeast)
1 ½ cups warm water
1 tablespoon salt
½ cup brown sugar
4 tablespoons shortening
½ cup molasses
1 ½ cups medium rye flour
5 to 6 cups all-purpose flour

In medium bowl soak raisins overnight in enough water to cover; drain. In large bowl dissolve yeast in warm water. Add salt, brown sugar, shortening and molasses. Stir to mix, then add raisins and rye flour. Stir in all-purpose flour. Form a ball, place in greased bowl and let rise until doubled. Punch down. Make 3 loaves, using standard size loaf pans, and let rise until almost double. Bake in 350-degree oven 1 hour. Turn out on rack to cool. Makes 3 loaves.

Mrs. Bill Mark, Independence, 1977

Garlic Parmesan Loaf

1 pkg. dry yeast
¼ cup warm water
2 cups milk
1 cup grated Parmesan cheese
2 tablespoons sugar
2 tablespoons oil
2 teaspoons salt
⅛ teaspoon cayenne pepper (approximately)
5 ½ cups sifted all-purpose flour (approximately)
   Melted butter
2 teaspoons garlic salt

In small bowl dissolve yeast in warm water. In saucepan or microwave container heat milk to almost simmering, then cool to lukewarm. Into large mixing bowl measure cheese, sugar, oil, salt and cayenne. Add milk and stir until sugar is dissolved. Gradually mix in 2 cups sifted flour to make moderately stiff dough. Turn out onto lighly floured surface and knead until smooth, 5 to 8 minutes. Shape into a ball. Place in greased bowl and grease surface of dough. Cover and let rise in warm place until doubled in size. Punch down. Divide dough in half, shaping each half into a ball. Cover each ball of dough and let rest 10 minutes. On lightly floured surface, roll out half of dough to 10x16-inch rectangle. Brush with melted butter and sprinkle with 1 teaspoon garlic salt. Cut into four 4x10-inch rectangles. Stack rectangles together, buttered side up. Cut into 5 stacks, 2 inches wide and 4 inches long. Arrange stacks in row, long cut side down, in greased 4½x8½-inch loaf pan. Repeat with remaining half of dough. Let rise in warm place until doubled. Bake in 400-degree oven 30 to 35 minutes or until done. Makes 2 loaves.

Sheryl Renner, Winfield, 1968

Greek Honey-Nut Bread

2 ½ to 3 cups all-purpose flour
1 pkg. active dry yeast
¾ cup milk
¼ cup granulated sugar
½ teaspoon salt
¼ cup butter or margarine
1 egg
½ teaspoon grated lemon peel (optional)
½ cup light or dark raisins
½ cup chopped figs
½ cup chopped walnuts
¼ cup honey

In large mixer bowl combine 1 cup flour and yeast. Heat milk, sugar, salt and butter just until warm (115 to 120 degrees), stirring constantly to melt butter. Add to dry mixture; add egg and lemon peel. Beat at low speed with electric mixer for ½ minute, scraping bowl. Beat 3 minutes at high speed. By hand, stir in enough remaining flour to make moderately stiff dough. Knead on floured surface until smooth, 5 to 10 minutes. Shape into ball. Place in greased 9x1½-inch round baking pan. Let rise until doubled, about 45 minutes. Knead in fruit and nuts. Bake in 375-degree oven about 30 minutes. Remove from pan; brush with honey. Makes 1 loaf.

Cynthia Lyne, Wichita, 1979

Sour Cream Twists

3 ½ cups sifted all-purpose flour
1 teaspoon salt
1 cup shortening (part butter)
1 cake compressed yeast (or 1 pkg. dry yeast)
1 cup thick sour cream
1 egg, well beaten
2 egg yolks
1 teaspoon vanilla
1 cup sugar (for sprinkling board and dough)

Sift flour before measuring. Sift together flour and salt into large mixing bowl. Cut in shortening with pastry blender, leaving some of shortening in lumps the size of giant peas. Add crumbled yeast, sour cream, well-beaten egg, egg yolks and vanilla. Mix thoroughly. Cover bowl with damp cloth and refrigerate for at least 2 hours. (The dough does not rise, but becomes very cold and rather firm.) Take out half of dough, leaving other half in bowl in refrigerator to roll out later. Sprinkle surface generously with part of the sugar (use half of sugar for first half of dough). Round up dough on sugared board. Then roll out into oblong about 8x16 inches. Fold the two ends to center, allowing one end to overlap the other. Sprinkle with sugar and roll out again to same size. Repeat process a third time. Roll out dough a little less than ¼ inch thick. Cut into stips about 1x4 inches. Twist ends of each strip in opposite directions, stretching dough gently and only slightly as you do so. Place twists on ungreased heavy baking sheet, pressing down ends to keep twists in shape. (They can be twisted in various shapes.) Bake immediately in 375-degree oven for about 15 minutes. When a very delicate brown, remove from oven and from baking sheet onto cooling rack. Repeat this process for other half of dough. Makes 5 to 6 dozen twists.

Note: This is really not a very complicated process but the directions are explicit. When baked, you can see the layers of dough with the sugar on them. The dough (before shaping) may be left in the refrigerator all night, and since it does not need to rise after shaping, it provides an easy, quick method for making a delicious snack.

Mrs. Russell Wynd, Arkansas City, 1955

Pancake Rolls

¾ cup milk
4 tablespoons sugar
1 pkg. yeast
⅓ cup lukewarm water
1 egg, beaten
½ cup shortening, melted
¼ teaspoon salt
2 ½ cups buttermilk pancake mix
1 ½ cups all-purpose flour

In saucepan or microwave container scald milk and add sugar. Cool. In large bowl combine milk mixture with yeast, water, beaten egg, melted shortening and salt. Add pancake mix. Blend well. Add flour gradually. When stiff enough, turn out onto floured board and knead until flour is all mixed in. Let rise until doubled in bulk. Form into rolls in greased round or square pans and let rise until double in bulk. Bake in 400-degree oven 15 to 20 minutes. Makes 2 to 3 dozen rolls.

Mrs. Clarence Smith, Wichita, 1963

Shortcut Pan Rolls

2 packets (0.8 oz. each) instant grits (½ cup total)
⅓ cup sugar
1 tablespoon salt
3 cups hot water
⅓ cup vegetable oil
6 to 6 ½ cups sifted all-purpose flour
2 pkgs. dry yeast
Butter

Combine instant grits, sugar and salt in large mixer bowl. Add water, oil and 2 cups flour. Beat 2 minutes on low speed of mixer. Add 1 cup additional flour and yeast. Beat 1 minute on low speed. Stir in enough additional flour to make soft dough. Turn out onto well-floured board or canvas. Knead until smooth and

Shortcut Pan Rolls — continued

elastic, about 10 minutes. Divide dough in half. Shape each half into 8 to 10 balls; place in 2 greased 8-inch round cake pans. Cover; let rise until nearly doubled in size. Bake in preheated 400-degree oven 30 to 35 minutes or until golden brown. Remove from pans; brush with butter. Serve warm. Makes 3 dozen rolls.

Lil Riedy, Wichita, 1979

Quick Sour Cream Rolls

    1 pkg. active dry yeast
    ¼ cup hot tap water
    2 ⅓ cups all-purpose flour
    2 tablespoons sugar
    1 teaspoon salt
    ¼ teaspoon soda
    1 cup dairy sour cream
    1 egg
      Butter

Grease 12 medium muffin cups. In large mixer bowl dissolve yeast in hot water. Add 1⅓ cups flour, then sugar, salt, soda, sour cream and egg. Blend ½ minute on low speed of mixer, scraping bowl constantly. Stir in remaining flour thoroughly. Divide batter evenly among muffin cups. Let rise in warm place 50 minutes. Batter will rise slightly but will not double. Heat oven to 350 degrees. Bake 30 minutes or until golden brown. Remove from pans immediately. If desired, brush tops of rolls with soft butter. Serve warm. Makes 1 dozen.

Note: If desired, batter can be spread evenly in cups and covered with greased waxed paper to let rise in refrigerator 6 to 24 hours before baking.

Mrs. James Overstreet, Newton, 1972

SANDWICHES

Mexican Beef Heroes

- **6 slices bacon**
- **½ lb. ground chuck**
- **½ cup onion, chopped**
- **1 can (4 oz.) green chilies, chopped**
- **½ cup ripe olives, chopped**
- **¼ cup ketchup**
- **½ teaspoon salt**
- **½ teaspoon chili powder**
- **6 steak buns**
- **6 slices (6 oz.) Colby cheese**
- **6 slices (6 oz.) Muenster cheese**

In skillet or microwave cook bacon until crisp; drain. In large skillet brown ground chuck and onion in small amount of bacon grease. Stir in green chilies, olives, ketchup, salt and chili powder; cook 5 minutes, stirring occasionally. Split buns in half lengthwise. Place a slice of Colby cheese, cut to fit, on bottom half of bun; top with ⅓ cup of meat mixture, bacon slice and slice of Muenster cheese cut to fit; press down gently with top half of bun. Wrap each sandwich in foil. Bake in 375-degree oven 10 minutes. If frozen for later use, thaw in refrigerator and add 5 minutes to baking time. Makes 6 big sandwiches.

I got this recipe from a friend with whom I share ideas, and use it to save time when the kids come home for a visit. I generally double the recipe.

Donna Louderback, Arkansas City, 1987

Sunshine in a Pocket

1 medium tomato
4 large pita bread rounds
6 eggs
⅓ cup milk
Salt and pepper
3 slices American cheese

Chop tomato. Cut bread in half to make pockets. Crack eggs and put into microwave-safe bowl. Stir in milk, salt and pepper. Cook in microwave on high for 4 minutes; stir. Tear cheese into small pieces. Sprinkle cheese over eggs. Cook on high for 1 to 2 minutes; stir. Fill each pita pocket with egg mixture. Top with tomato. Makes 2 to 4 servings.

Raymond C. Miller, Bentley, 1987

Tuna Long Johns

1 cup drained tuna (about 2 6½-oz. cans)
1 cup grated cheddar cheese
2 tablespoons chopped celery
2 tablespoons chopped onion
2 tablespoons sweet pickle or pickle relish
3 hard-cooked eggs, cut up
Salad dressing
8 hot dog or hamburger buns

In large bowl combine tuna, cheese, celery, onion, relish, eggs and salad dressing. Fill either 8 hot dog buns or 8 hamburger buns with mixture. Wrap individually in aluminum foil. Place on cookie sheet and bake in 250-degree oven 30 minutes. Makes 8 sandwiches.

Audrey Pitonak, Wichita, 1986

Pizza Planks

> 1 loaf (12 inches) French bread
> 1 jar (12 oz.) spaghetti sauce
> 1 pkg. (4 oz.) sliced pepperoni
> 1 jar (2 ½ oz.) sliced mushrooms, drained
> 12 oz. shredded mozzarella cheese
> 2 tablespoons grated Parmesan cheese

Place bread on cutting board. Carefully split bread in half lengthwise. Remove some of soft bread to make slightly hollowed loaf. Place each half on plate, cut sides up. Spoon spaghetti sauce evenly over both halves. Arrange pepperoni, mushrooms and mozzarella cheese evenly over the tops. Sprinkle with Parmesan cheese. Microwave each pizza separately on high 1½ minutes. Rotate plate a quarter turn. Microwave on high another 1 to 1½ minutes, until cheese is bubbly.

In conventional oven, place pizza planks on baking sheet and bake in preheated 350-degree oven 10 minutes or until cheese is bubbly. Makes 4 servings.

My mother taught me how to make this when I was 10 years old. It can be a quick lunch, or, if the recipe is halved, a delicious snack. Other ingredients such as green peppers, onions, cooked sausage and hot dogs can be used.

Christy Aeschliman, Wichita, 1988

Salmon Rolls

> 1 can (16 oz.) salmon
> ½ medium onion, chopped
> Salt and pepper
> 2 ¼ cups prepared biscuit mix
> ⅔ cup milk

Drain salmon; place in bowl and mix throughly with chopped onion, salt and pepper. Combine biscuit mix and milk to make soft dough. Turn onto surface well dusted with baking mix. Shape into ball; knead several times. Roll ½-inch thick on floured board. Spread with salmon mixture and roll up as for jelly roll. Cut into 1-

Salmon Rolls — continued

inch slices and bake on ungreased cookie sheet in 400-degree oven 10 to 20 minutes. Makes 8 to 10 rolls.

May be served with creamed peas or other creamed vegetable, and a salad.

Katie Funk Wiebe, Hillsboro, 1990

Skillet Beef Scramble

   ¼ **cup butter**
   ¾ **cup sliced onions**
1 ½ **lbs. ground beef**
   2 **teaspoons salt**
   ½ **teaspoon pepper**
   ¼ **cup all-purpose flour**
1 ⅔ **cups evaporated milk**
   ¾ **cup ketchup**
   2 **tablespoons parsley flakes**
   8 **hamburger buns, toasted**
     Green pepper rings (for garnish)

Preheat electric skillet to 300 degrees. Melt butter in skillet. Add onions and cook 5 minutes. Add ground beef, salt and pepper, breaking up meat with a fork. Increase temperature to 350 degrees and cook 10 minutes. Reduce heat to 225 degrees. Blend in flour. Gradually stir in evaporated milk. Continue cooking until mixture is thickened, stirring occasionally. Stir in ketchup and parsley. Heat 2 minutes. Serve over toasted buns. Garnish with green pepper rings, if desired. Makes 8 servings.

Marie S. Johnson, Wichita, 1976

New Jersey Hoagies

1 can (15 ½ oz.) spaghetti sauce
2 tablespoons dark brown sugar
3 tablespoons lemon juice
¼ cup minced onion
1 teaspoon salt
2 teaspoons prepared mustard
¼ teaspoon Worcestershire sauce
   Broiled flank steak
   Large crusty rolls

In small saucepan mix spaghetti sauce, brown sugar, lemon juice, onion, salt, mustard and Worcestershire sauce. Bring to boil over moderate heat. Reduce heat and cook gently about 5 minutes. (Makes 1¾ cups sauce.) Slice steak thinly, across grain, and sandwich it and some of hot sauce into rolls. Makes 6 servings.

Betty McJunkin, Toronto, 1963

Hash and Cheese Grill

1 can (16 oz.) corned beef hash
⅓ cup ketchup
¾ teaspoon oregano
1 teaspoon parsley flakes
2 teaspoons instant minced onion
4 English muffins, split and buttered
8 slices American cheese, cut into strips

In medium bowl mix hash, ketchup, oregano, parsley and onion. Spread evenly on muffin halves. Top with cheese strips. Broil 8 to 10 inches from heat until cheese melts and hash mixture is hot and bubbly. Makes 8 open-face sandwiches.

Bernard Jacobson, Atchison, 1978

Hamburgers Italiano

1 ½ lbs. ground beef
 4 tablespoons tomato paste
 ¼ cup finely chopped onion
   Cumin
   Oregano
   Salt and pepper
   Garlic salt
   Parmesan cheese
 4 slices mozzarella cheese
 1 loaf French bread
   Olive oil
   Lettuce
 1 tomato, sliced

Divide ground beef into 4 parts, 2 a little larger than the others. Pat out into 8x1-inch patties, making a ½-inch ridge on the edge of the 2 large patties. Into the "bowls" thus formed spread tomato paste and onion. Sprinkle to taste with cumin, oregano, salt, pepper, garlic salt and Parmesan cheese. Place smaller patties on top and seal edges. Broil 3 inches from heat 15 to 20 minutes. Place 2 mozzarella cheese slices on top of each patty and broil until melted. To prepare bread, slice loaf of French bread lengthwise, but not completely through. Scoop out about half of "pulp" of loaf and cut loaf in half crosswise. Brush inside of each half with olive oil. Place patty on each half and add lettuce and tomato. Serves 2 generously, or cut each sandwich in half to serve 4.

Patricia Langworthy, Derby, 1964

Tuna Pasties

1 can (7 oz.) tuna, drained and flaked
1 cup shredded cheddar cheese
¼ cup chopped celery
1 tablespoon chopped parsley
⅓ cup dairy sour cream
1 pkg. (8 oz.) refrigerated biscuits
1 tablespoon butter or margarine, melted

In small bowl combine tuna, cheese, celery, parsley and sour cream. Pat or roll each biscuit into 3x4-inch oval. Place half of biscuits on greased baking sheet. Place about ⅓ cup tuna mixture on each biscuit. Top with remaining biscuits and seal edges with a fork. Brush tops with butter. Let stand 15 minutes. Bake in 400-degree oven 15 to 18 minutes or until golden brown. Makes 5 to 6 servings.

Mrs. Leo Schaeffer, Larned, 1973

Toasted Salmon Sandwiches

⅓ cup butter or margarine, melted
12 slices white bread
1 can (6 oz.) salmon
1 pkg. (10 oz.) frozen peas, cooked and drained
¼ cup instant minced onion
1 can (10 ½ oz.) condensed cream of mushroom soup
4 eggs
2 cups milk

About 1½ hours before serving, preheat oven to 325 degrees. Brush melted butter or margarine on 1 side of each bread slice and arrange 6 slices, buttered side up, in layer in well-buttered 9x13-inch baking dish. In medium bowl flake salmon. Stir in peas and onions. Spread mixture evenly over bread slices in pan. Cover with remaining bread slices, buttered side up. In another bowl beat undiluted soup, eggs and milk until blended. Slowly pour over and around bread. Bake in preheated oven 1 hour or until knife inserted in custard comes out clean. Serve at once. Makes 6 servings.

Judy Fitzgeralds, Herrington, 1977

Poor Man's Barbecue

1 whole bologna (2 to 3 lbs.)
3 tablespoons pickle relish
½ cup grated cheddar cheese
Several slices salt pork or bacon
Buttered buns
Barbecue sauce

Slice bologna in half lengthwise. With a curved grapefruit knife or the edge of a spoon, hollow out center of each half of bologna to make a shell about 1½ inches thick. Grind bologna taken from hollowed-out portion. In large bowl mix ground meat, relish and grated cheese. Pack all of mixture into half of bologna, mounding it up as necessary. Top with second half of bologna and press firmly together. Tie twine around each end of bologna to hold halves together. Wrap several slices of salt pork or bacon around outside of bologna. Tie with twine at 1½-inch intervals. Put bologna on spit, making sure one tine of each fork goes into each half. Spit-barbecue roll over medium heat until bacon is crisp and meat is heated through, about 20 to 30 minutes. Slice and serve on buttered buns topped with barbecue sauce. Makes 12 to 15 servings.

Mrs. Newton Breth, Wichita, 1964

Beef Bologna Pizza-Style

2 lbs. lean ground chuck
1 cup water
2 tablespoons quick curing salt
1 ½ teaspoons liquid smoke
½ teaspoon garlic powder
¼ teaspoon onion powder
2 tablespoons oregano
1 cup chopped sweet red and green peppers
1 cup shredded longhorn cheese

In bowl mix chuck, water, curing salt, liquid smoke, garlic powder, onion powder and oregano, using hands. Pat out into large rectangle. Sprinkle peppers and cheese evenly on meat. Roll up jelly-roll fashion into 2 rolls, sealing ends. Wrap in plastic wrap and refrigerate 24 hours. Remove wrap and bake uncovered on rack over shallow pan in 300-degree oven 1 hour. Let cool completely, then slice thin to serve.

Delma Carter, Wichita, 1977

Bacon Salad Sandwiches

4 strips bacon, cooked and chopped
2 cups grated cabbage
¼ cup minced green pepper
½ cup chopped tomato
½ cup salad dressing
   Salt and pepper to taste
8 slices toast spread with salad dressing

In large bowl combine bacon bits, cabbage, green pepper, tomato and salad dressing. Season with salt and pepper. Spread filling on toast, using 2 slices per sandwich. Makes 4 sandwiches.

Mrs. Melo Melichar, Caldwell, 1975

Avocado Sandwich Spread

 1 **large avocado**
   Juice of 1 small lemon
 1 **small onion, minced**
 1 **small tomato, peeled and minced**
 2 **small sour pickles, minced**
 1 **garlic clove, mashed, or garlic salt to taste**
 ⅛ **teaspoon salt (if garlic clove is used)**
 ⅓ **cup minced pecans**
   Bread

In medium bowl mash avocado as you would a potato, then add lemon juice to avoid discoloration of avocado. Add minced onion, tomato, pickles, mashed garlic or garlic salt and minced pecans. Mix well and spread on lightly buttered bread (white or wheat). Makes 4 to 6 sandwiches.

Evelyn McEntire, Wichita, 1962

Super Sandwich Spread

 1 **pkg. (3 oz.) dried beef, finely cut**
 3 **oz. longhorn cheese, shredded**
 2 **tablespoons quick-cooking tapioca**
 1 **can (15 oz.) tomato herb sauce**
 2 **tablespoons finely chopped onion or onion flakes**

In medium bowl combine dried beef, cheese, tapioca, tomato sauce and onion. Let stand 30 minutes. Cook in double broiler or in greased glass baking dish in 350-degree oven 30 minutes. Stir twice. Makes filling for 10 to 12 sandwiches. May be served hot or cold. Also, sandwiches may be made using buns, then wrapped in foil and frozen. Heat frozen sandwiches in 250-degree oven 45 minutes. Also may be used on crackers for appetizers. Keeps well in refrigerator.

Mrs. Paul Bennett, Hutchinson, 1978

DESSERTS

Ask for one favorite recipe and every cook is likely to select a dessert creation, probably chocolate.

Without exception, recipes submitted for cakes, pies and other desserts have outnumbered the entries in any other contest category.

The bundt pan was a novel piece of equipment in 1955; today it is a kitchen standard. Cakes baked in the standard loaf pan never go out of fashion in Kansas.

Each year more cooks submit more dessert recipes to be prepared in the microwave oven, which was an expensive novelty appliance in 1955.

Cheesecakes and frozen desserts are popular with Kansans — homemade ice cream, sherbet and frozen pies. Apples are the favorite fruit to use in a cake or pie. Kansans also have a love affair with rhubarb.

And desserts with odd ingredients — sauerkraut and beets — have been Favorite Recipe Contest winners.

CAKES

Rhubarb Kuchen

- 2 cups all-purpose flour
- 1 teaspoon soda
- ¼ teaspoon salt
- ½ cup brown sugar
- ½ cup shortening
- 1 egg, well beaten
- 1 teaspoon vanilla
- 1 cup buttermilk or sour milk
- ½ to 2 cups finely cut rhubarb

Topping
- ½ cup brown sugar
- 2 tablespoons flour
- 2 teaspoons cinnamon
- 2 tablespoons melted butter
- 1 cup pecan pieces

In medium bowl combine flour, soda and salt; stir or sift. In large bowl cream sugar and shortening; add egg and vanilla; add buttermilk or sour milk alternately with sifted dry ingredients; fold in rhubarb. Spread in a greased 9x13-inch pan. For topping combine in small bowl brown sugar, flour, cinnamon, melted butter and pecans; sprinkle over batter. Bake in 350-degree oven 35 to 40 minutes.

Judi Pavelski, Wichita, 1986

Applesauce Cake-in-a-Jar

⅔ cup shortening
2 ⅔ cups sugar
4 eggs
2 cups applesauce
⅔ cup water
3 ⅓ cups all-purpose flour
2 teaspoons soda
1 teaspoon cinnamon
⅔ cup nuts (optional)
½ teaspoon baking powder
1 ½ teaspoons salt
2 teaspoons ground cloves
8 1-pint tapered canning jars with wide-mouth lids, or 6
1 ½-pint tapered canning jars, or 4 1-quart tapered
canning jars

In large bowl cream shortening with sugar. Beat in eggs, apple-sauce and water. Sift together flour, soda and cinnamon. Blend dry ingredients into applesauce mixture. Pour into well-greased jars, filling ½ to ⅔ full. Bake in 325-degree oven 45 minutes. Using insulated mitts to protect hands, remove 1 jar at a time, wipe seal edge clean, and put on dry canning lid and ring. (If cake has risen higher than the jar, slice off the top of the cake, so there is head-space of ¼ to ½ inch.) Screw rings tightly. Jar will seal as cake cools. May be stored as canned goods for 6 months. (For longer storage refrigerate or freeze.) To serve, remove from jar and slice. Serve plain or garnish with a dollop of whipped cream. A cherry or pecan half will dress it up even more.

This recipe makes a great gift. It is similar to some of the high-priced specialty gifts you find in the store. I got the recipe from a friend in Iowa this summer and have enjoyed using it. I make a little "cap" of fabric to decorate the jar.

Elaine Clark, Wellington, 1990

Nutty Cakes

¼ cup butter or margarine
⅓ cup peanut butter
1 cup sugar
2 eggs, well beaten
1 teaspoon vanilla
1 cup mashed cooked carrots
½ cup broken pecans
½ cup flaked coconut (optional)
2 tablespoons grated orange rind
¼ cup orange juice
½ cup milk
2 cups sifted all-purpose flour
2 teaspoons baking powder
¼ teaspoon soda
½ teaspoon salt
　Maple frosting

In large bowl cream butter and peanut butter until thoroughly blended. Gradually add sugar, mixing well. Add beaten eggs. Mix until smooth and creamy. Add vanilla, carrots, pecans, coconut, orange rind, orange juice and milk. Mix well. Sift together flour, baking powder, soda and salt. Add to creamed mixture. Mix well. Place paper baking cups in muffin pans and fill ½ full. Bake 20 to 25 minutes in 350-degree oven. Frost with maple frosting. Makes about 24 cupcakes.

Mrs. John W. Green, Clifton, 1963

Poke and Pour Gingerbread

    2 ¼ cups all-purpose flour
      ¾ cup brown sugar
      1 teaspoon baking powder
      ½ teaspoon baking soda
      ½ teaspoon salt
      2 teaspoons cinnamon
      1 teaspoon ginger
      ¼ teaspoon cloves
      ½ teaspoon nutmeg
      ¾ cup light molasses
      ¾ cup oil
      ¾ cup water
      2 eggs
Topping
      1 cup brown sugar
      ½ cup margarine
      ⅓ cup water

Combine flour, brown sugar, baking powder, soda, salt, cinnamon, ginger, cloves, nutmeg, molasses, oil, water and eggs in large mixing bowl. Stir until moistened, then beat at medium speed 3 minutes. Pour into greased 9x13-inch pan. Bake in 350-degree oven 30 to 35 minutes. Just before gingerbread is done, combine brown sugar, margarine and water in saucepan and bring to boil. Remove gingerbread from oven, poke holes all over it with a long-tined fork and pour topping over hot cake. Good with whipped topping. Makes 10 generous servings.

Our oldest grandson loves gingerbread, so I like to try different recipes for him.

Dorothy Frey, Fredonia, 1986

Coconut-Peach Upside-Down Cake (Microwave)

3 tablespoons melted butter or margarine
¼ cup flaked coconut
½ cup packed brown sugar
1 can (8 oz.) drained sliced peaches
1 pkg. (9 oz.) yellow cake mix

Melt butter or margarine in a 10-inch microwave-safe round baking dish. Add coconut and brown sugar and mix well. Arrange drained peach slices on top of butter mixture in an even design. Mix yellow cake batter as package directs. Spread batter over peaches. Microwave 7 minutes on simmer; microwave 3 to 4 minutes on high or until a toothpick comes out clean. Let stand 1 minute, then invert onto serving platter. Serve with whipped topping or ice cream. Makes 8 to 10 servings.

Twice the Eagle judges have chosen my microwave upside-down cakes. So it has become a tradition to find new ones to submit each year!

Joan C. Chance, Mount Hope, 1988

Sunshine Cake

        1 cup sifted cake flour
    1 ½ teaspoons baking powder
        ½ teaspoon salt
        ¼ cup oil
        3 egg yolks
        ½ cup unsweeted frozen orange juice
          Sugar substitute to equal 1/2 cup sugar
        4 egg whites
        ½ teaspoon cream of tartar

Sift together flour, baking powder and salt. Make a well in dry mixture and add, in order, oil, unbeaten egg yolks, orange juice concentrate and sugar substitute. Beat until smooth. Add cream of tartar to egg whites and beat until stiff; add egg mixture to beaten whites and gently fold until blended. Do not overmix. Pour into 9-inch tube pan. Bake in 325-degree oven 35 minutes. Makes 10 servings.

Note: suitable for diabetic diet.

Patsy Herrman, Garden Plain, 1984

Poor Man's Chocolate Cake

        3 cups all-purpose flour
        2 cups sugar
        ¼ cup cocoa
        1 teaspoon salt
        2 teaspoons soda
        ¾ cup oil
        2 cups cold water
        2 tablespoons lemon juice

In mixing bowl combine flour, sugar, cocoa, salt, soda, oil and water. Mix well; add lemon juice and stir to mix. Pour into greased and floured 9x13-inch pan or 10x15-inch jelly roll pan. Bake in 350-degree oven 30 to 35 minutes. Serve warm or cooled. Makes 12 to 15 servings.

Dorothy Gerkin, Piedmont, 1988

Carrot-Yogurt Squares

```
    1 cup honey
   ¾ cup oil
    1 cup plain yogurt
    2 eggs
    1 cup whole-wheat flour
    1 cup all-purpose flour
    2 teaspoons baking powder
   ¼ teaspoon salt
1 ½ teaspoons cinnamon
    1 cup grated carrots
    1 cup chopped nuts
    1 cup raisins
Frosting
    1 pkg. (3 oz.) cream cheese, softened
    3 cups confectioners' sugar
   ¼ teaspoon salt
    2 to 3 tablespoons milk
    1 teaspoon vanilla
```

Heat oven to 350 degrees; grease 9x13-inch cake pan. In large bowl combine honey, oil, yogurt and eggs; beat well. Lightly spoon flours into measuring cup and level off. Add flours, baking powder, salt and cinnamon to liquid mixture; blend well. Stir in carrots, nuts and raisins; mix well. Pour into prepared pan. Bake in 350-degree oven 30 to 40 minutes. Frost when cool.

Frosting: In a small bowl beat cream cheese. Beat confectioners' sugar, salt, milk and vanilla into cream cheese until frosting is smooth and creamy. If necessary, thin with additional milk to spreading consistency. Refrigerate leftovers. Makes 36 bars.

Sharon Sherwood, Wichita, 1989

Cranberry Nut Pound Cake

2 sticks (1 cup) margarine
2 cups granulated sugar
4 eggs
½ cup evaporated milk
1 teaspoon vanilla
2 cups all-purpose flour
1 cup chopped raw cranberries
1 cup chopped nuts

In large bowl cream margarine; add sugar, 1 cup at at time, continuing to mix. Add eggs, one at a time, mixing after each addition. Stir in evaporated milk and vanilla; blend in flour. Add chopped cranberries and nuts to batter and pour into greased and floured tube pan. Bake at 350 degrees until cake is golden brown, about 1 hour. Let cake stand on cooling rack 15 minutes, then invert pan on serving plate.

Note: no baking powder or soda needed.

Barbara Burkett, Madison, 1989

Surprise Lemon-Orange Bundt Cake

1 **pkg. yellow cake mix (2-layer size)**
1 **pkg. (3 oz.) instant lemon pudding**
¼ **cup oil**
4 **eggs**
1 **cup water**
¼ **cup frozen orange juice concentrate, thawed**
1 ¾ **cups wheat germ (divided use)**
   1 **tablespoon grated lemon or orange peel**
   2 **tablespoons sugar**
   1 **tablespoon melted margarine**
Orange Icing-Glaze
   2 **cups confectioners' sugar**
   1 **tablespoon orange juice concentrate**
   1 **tablespoon melted butter or margarine**
   1 **teaspoon grated orange rind**
   2 **to 3 tablespoons warm water**

In a large bowl mix yellow cake mix and pudding mix. Add oil, eggs, water and juice concentrate. Mix according to directions on cake box. Add 1½ cups toasted wheat germ and orange peel. To toast wheat germ, place in shallow pan in 300-degree oven, sprinkle with 2 tablespoons sugar and 1 tablespoon melted margarine. Stir once or twice until toasted; do not overbake. Grease and flour bundt pan, using margarine or butter; sprinkle with remaining ¼ cup wheat germ, coating sides if possible. Carefully pour batter into prepared pan. Bake in 350-degree oven 55 to 60 minutes. Cool 3 to 5 minutes; invert on plate. Ice with thin lemon-orange icing if desired: Combine confectioners' sugar, orange juice concentrate, butter or margarine and grated orange rind. Add water slowly until icing is desired consistency. Makes about 1½ cups glaze. Serves about 12.

Barbara Livingston, Cottonwood Falls, 1984

Oatmeal Chocolate-Chip Cake

1 ¾ cups boiling water
1 cup uncooked oatmeal
½ cup (1 stick) margarine or butter
1 cup brown sugar
1 cup granulated sugar
2 large or 3 small eggs
1 ¾ cups all-purpose flour
1 teaspoon baking soda
½ teaspoon salt
1 tablespoon cocoa
¾ cup pecans or walnuts (optional)
1 pkg. (12 oz.) semisweet chocolate chips

Pour boiling water over oatmeal in small bowl and let stand 10 minutes. Add to margarine and sugars combined in large bowl. Stir until margarine is melted. Add eggs and mix well. Sift together flour, baking soda, salt and cocoa. Add to sugar mixture and mix well. Stir in pecans or walnuts and about ½ package of chocolate chips. Pour batter into greased and floured 9x13-inch pan. Sprinkle remaining chips over top of batter. Bake at 350 degrees 35 to 40 minutes. Makes 20 to 24 servings.

This is a very easy cake to make and children especially enjoy it.

Denise Richards, Wichita, 1989

Orange Slice Fruit Cake

1 cup brown sugar
1 cup white sugar
1 cup butter or margarine
2 eggs, well beaten
1 can (15 to 16 oz.) applesauce
4 cups all-purpose flour
½ teaspoon salt
2 teaspoons soda
1 teaspoon cinnamon
1 teaspoon cloves
1 teaspoon allspice
1 cup chopped nuts
1 lb. dates, chopped
1 lb. orange slice candy, chopped

In large bowl cream sugars and butter; add eggs and apple-sauce. Beat well. Combine 3 cups flour with salt, soda, cinnamon, cloves and allspice. Add to creamed mixture. Dredge nuts, dates and candy in remaining 1 cup flour and fold into mixture. Bake in well-greased 10-inch tube pan in 275-degree oven 2½ hours. Makes about 20 servings.

Note: This cake need not be aged, but it keeps well.

Mrs. H.E. Gamble Jr., Wichita, 1969

German Fruit Cake

¾ cup butter or margarine
2 cups sugar
4 eggs
3 cups sifted all-purpose flour
½ teaspoon allspice
½ teaspoon nutmeg
1 teaspoon soda
1 cup buttermilk
⅔ cup cherry preserves
⅔ cup apricot preserves
⅔ cup pineapple preserves
1 cup chopped pecans
½ teaspoon vanilla

In large bowl cream butter and sugar together; add eggs. Sift together flour and spices. Add soda to buttermilk, then add to creamed mixture alternately with dry ingredients. Fold in preserves, pecans and vanilla. Pour into 10-inch greased tube pan pan or 2 greased loaf pans. Bake 1½ hours in 325-degree oven. Let cool 15 minutes before removing from pans. Makes about 20 servings.

Mrs. Alfred Luna, Big Bow, 1964

Green Apple Cake

> 1 cup butter or margarine
> 2 cups sugar
> 2 eggs
> 2 ½ cups sifted all-purpose flour
> 2 teaspoons baking powder
> 1 teaspoon soda
> 3 cups tart apple slices (peeled)
> ¾ cup chopped nuts

Glaze

> 1 cup confectioners' sugar
> 1 tablespoon corn syrup
> 1 tablespoon butter or margarine
> 1 tablespoon milk

In large bowl cream butter or margarine and sugar until light and fluffy. Add eggs and beat well. Add flour, baking powder and soda and mix well. Add apples and nuts. Batter will be thick; no liquid is needed. Spread in greased 9x13-inch pan and bake in 350-degree oven for 1 hour. Glaze while still hot: In small bowl combine confectioners' sugar, corn syrup, butter and milk. Pour evenly over cake. Makes 12 to 15 servings.

Mrs. W.I. Potteiger, Fort Scott, 1972

Kraut Surprise Cake

⅔ cup butter
1 ½ cups sugar
3 eggs
1 teaspoon vanilla
½ cup cocoa
2 ¼ cups sifted all-purpose flour
1 teaspoon baking powder
1 teaspoon soda
¼ teaspoon salt
1 cup water
⅔ cup chopped sauerkraut, rinsed and drained
Confectioners' sugar, whipped cream or mocha cream
(optional)
Mocha Cream
1 ½ cups heavy cream
3 tablespoons sugar
1 tablespoon instant coffee
2 teaspoons cocoa
1 teaspoon rum (optional)

In large bowl cream butter with sugar. Beat in eggs, one at a time. Add vanilla. Sift together cocoa, flour, baking powder, soda and salt and add to creamed mixture alternately with water. Stir in kraut. Turn into 2 greased 8-inch round pans lined with waxed paper. Bake in 350-degree oven 30 minutes or until cake tests done. Dust with confectioners' sugar, or put layers together with whipped cream or mocha cream. For mocha cream, combine cream, sugar, instant coffee and cocoa in medium mixing bowl; whip until soft peaks form; whip in rum, if desired. Makes 12 servings.

Mrs. H. Allen Miller, Sylvia, 1965

Cocoa Apple Cake

- **3 eggs**
- **2 cups sugar**
- **1 cup margarine**
- **½ cup water**
- **2 ½ cups all-purpose flour**
- **2 tablespoons cocoa**
- **1 teaspoon baking soda**
- **1 teaspoon cinnamon**
- **1 teaspoon allspice**
- **1 cup finely chopped nuts**
- **½ cup chocolate pieces**
- **2 apples, cored and finely chopped**
- **1 tablespoon vanilla**

In large bowl beat together eggs, sugar, margarine and water until fluffy. Sift together flour, cocoa, soda, cinnamon and allspice. Add to creamed mixture and mix well. Fold in nuts, chocolate pieces, apples and vanilla until evenly distributed. Spoon into greased and floured 10-inch tube pan. Bake in 325-degree oven 60 to 70 mintues or until cake tests done. Makes 10 servings.

Vicky Peterson, Derby, 1977

Sour Cream Raisin Cake

1 ½ cups seedless raisins
2 cups sifted all-purpose flour
1 ½ cups granulated sugar
½ cup cocoa
1 teaspoon cinnamon
1 teaspoon ground cloves
½ teaspoon nutmeg
1 teaspoon salt
1 teaspoon baking soda
1 cup black walnuts
1 cup thick sour cream
2 eggs
3 tablespoons shortening, melted, or salad oil
2 teaspoons vanilla
Chocolate butter frosting with peanut butter (optional)

Preheat oven to 325 degrees. Grease and flour 8-inch tube pan. Rinse raisins; drain; snip with scissors. Into large bowl sift together flour, sugar, cocoa, cinnamon, cloves, nutmeg, salt and soda. Mix in raisins and nuts. Add sour cream, eggs, shortening or salad oil and vanilla all at once; beat well. Pour into tube pan. Bake 1¼ hours or until cake tester comes out clean. Invert onto a wire cake rack for about 5 minutes. Loosen cake and remove from pan. Frost with chocolate butter frosting with 2 teaspoons peanut butter added, if desired. Makes 16 servings.

Mrs. F.C. Lankenau, Winfield, 1955

Easy Pineapple Cake

2 cups all-purpose flour
2 cups sugar
2 teaspoons soda
1 can (20 oz.) crushed pineapple (do not drain)
Topping
⅔ cup (1 small can) evaporated milk
1 stick margarine (½ cup)
¾ cup sugar
½ cup nuts (optional)

In large bowl combine flour, sugar, soda and pineapple. Pour into greased 9x13-inch cake pan. Bake in 350-degree oven 45 minutes. Remove from oven and pour on topping, which has been prepared by combining evaporated milk, margarine and sugar in a saucepan; bring mixture to boil and boil hard 5 minutes. Stir in nuts before pouring over cake. Makes 12 to 16 servings.

Mrs. John White, Wichita, 1975

Westhaven Cake

1 pkg. (8 oz.) dates, chopped
1 cup hot water
1 cup sugar
½ cup butter or margarine
1 teaspoon vanilla
1 teaspoon soda
1 ¾ cups all-purpose flour
2 eggs
1 pkg. (12 oz.) chocolate chips
½ cup chopped nuts

In small bowl mix dates and hot water; let stand until cool. In large bowl combine sugar, butter or margarine, vanilla, soda, flour and eggs; mix well. Add date mixture. Pour batter into 9x12-inch pan; sprinkle chocolate chips and nuts on top. Bake 30 minutes in 350-degree oven. Makes 9 to 12 servings.

Mrs. Wesley Capers, Wichita, 1955

Brown Sugar Pound Cake

1 cup butter or margarine, softened
½ cup shortening
1 lb. light brown sugar
1 cup sugar
5 eggs
3 cups all-purpose flour
1 cup milk
1 teaspoon vanilla
1 cup chopped pecans
Nut Glaze
1 cup sifted confectioners' sugar
2 tablespoons butter or margarine
6 tablespoons milk
½ teaspoon vanilla
½ cup nuts

In large bowl beat butter and shortening together. Gradually add sugars, creaming until mixture is light. Beat in eggs, one at a time. Sift flour and add to creamed mixture alternately with milk and vanilla. Stir in pecans. Pour batter into greased and floured 10-inch tube pan. Bake at 350 degrees 1 hour and 15 minutes. Remove from pan. In small bowl cream sugar and butter. Add milk, vanilla and nuts; mix well. Pour nut glaze over hot cake. Makes 12 to 14 servings.

Vickie Walker, Wichita, 1970

Syrian Nutmeg Cake

2 cups brown sugar
2 cups sifted all-purpose flour
½ cup margarine
½ cup finely chopped almonds
1 cup sour cream
1 teaspoon soda
1 egg
1 teaspoon nutmeg

In large bowl mix brown sugar, flour and margarine until fine and crumbly. Press ¼ of mixture into well-greased 8- or 9-inch

Syrian Nutmeg Cake — continued

pan. Sprinkle with half of almonds. In large bowl mix sour cream and soda; add egg, remaining crumbs and nutmeg; blend well. Pour over mixture in pan. Sprinkle with remaining almonds. Bake at 325 degrees about 40 to 50 minutes. Makes 4 to 6 servings.

Winifred S. Burden, Wichita, 1975

Golden Dollar Angel Cake

Angel Batter
- ½ cup sifted cake flour
- ¾ cup sifted sugar
- 6 egg whites
- ¾ teaspoon cream of tartar
- ¼ teaspoon salt
- ½ teaspoon vanilla
- ¼ teaspoon almond extract

Golden Batter
- ¾ cup sifted cake flour
- 1 teaspoon baking powder
- 6 egg yolks
- ¾ cup sugar
- ¼ teaspoon salt
- ½ teaspoon vanilla
- ½ teaspoon lemon extract
- ¼ cup boiling water

For angel batter, sift flour and sugar separately four times; set aside. In large bowl beat egg whites until frothy; add cream of tartar and salt; beat until mixture stands in peaks. Add sugar gradually. Add flavoring. Fold in flour. Pour into ungreased tube pan and let stand while preparing golden batter.

Sift together flour and baking powder. Beat egg yolks until lemon-colored and fluffy. Add sugar and salt, beating continuously. Add flavorings. Fold in flour mixture alternately with hot water. Pour slowly over angel batter. Bake in preheated 350-degree oven 30 to 35 minutes. Invert pan until cool. Frost and serve or use as an angel food or sponge cake.

Note: For high altitudes or high humidity, increase oven temperature to 375 degrees.

Mrs. Marvin Peterson, Concordia, 1969

PIES

Harvest Pie

- 1 **bag (12 oz.) cranberries**
- 1 **can (8 oz.) crushed pineapple, drained; reserve ¼ cup pineapple juice**
- 1 **cup brown sugar**
- ½ **cup white sugar**
- 3 **tablespoons all-purpose flour**
- 2 **tablespoons butter**
- ½ **cup broken pecans**
- ¼ **teaspoon salt**
- ½ **teaspoon almond extract**
- **Pastry for 9-inch, 2-crust pie**
- **Whole pecans for top**

In saucepan combine cranberries with ¼ cup pineapple juice, brown sugar and white sugar. (No water is needed.) Cook until cranberries are hot, stirring constantly. Add flour mixed with pineapple, butter, broken pecans, salt and almond extract. Pour into unbaked crust. Place lattice crust on top. Bake at 425 degrees 25 minutes. Place whole pecans in the holes of lattice, then bake at 350 degrees 10 minutes longer.

Helen Nixon, Emporia, 1985

Frozen Peanut Butter Pie

1 pkg. (8 oz.) cream cheese, softened
½ cup peanut butter
1 cup confectioners' sugar
½ cup milk
1 carton (8 or 9 oz.) frozen non-dairy whipped topping, thawed
1 (9-inch) graham cracker crust

In large bowl whip cheese until soft and fluffy. Beat in peanut butter and sugar. Slowly add milk, blending thoroughly. Fold topping into mixture. Pour into prepared crust. Freeze until firm. Wrap airtight with plastic wrap, then foil. This may be prepared 3 weeks ahead of time. Makes 8 servings.

We usually have many guests during the Kansas State Fair, and this is one item I always make ahead of time. It never fails to draw compliments.

Phyllis Hirst, Hutchinson, 1986

Sour Cream Lemon Pie

1 cup sugar
3 tablespoons cornstarch
¼ cup butter or margarine
1 tablespoon lemon rind
¼ cup lemon juice
1 cup milk
3 egg yolks, slightly beaten
1 cup sour cream
1 9-inch pie shell, baked
1 cup whipping cream, whipped

Combine sugar and cornstarch in 1½-quart saucepan. Add butter, lemon rind, lemon juice, milk and egg yolks. Cook and stir over medium heat until mixture comes to boil and is thickened. Remove from heat and fold in sour cream. Pour into 9-inch baked and cooled pie shell. Top with whipped cream. Refrigerate. Makes 6 servings.

Nancy Kopp, Manhattan, 1981

Swiss Apple Pie

5 medium apples, pared and cored
¾ cup sugar
½ teaspoon nutmeg
¾ teaspoon cinnamon
½ teaspoon salt
2 eggs, slightly beaten
1 cup evaporated milk
1 9-inch pastry shell, unbaked

Grind apples through medium knife of food chopper or chop in food processor (there should be about 2 cups). Mix with sugar, nutmeg, cinnamon, salt, eggs and milk. Pour into 9-inch pan lined with unbaked pastry shell. Bake 15 minutes at 450 degrees, then in 350-degree oven for 35 minutes longer or until firm.

Mrs. John F. Schaeffer, Newton, 1976

English Apple Pie

1 egg
½ teaspoon vanilla flavoring
¾ cup sugar
½ cup all-purpose flour
1 teaspoon baking powder
¼ teaspoon salt
1 cup chopped apples
½ cup chopped nuts
  Whipped cream

In large bowl beat egg. Add vanilla. Add sugar, flour, baking powder and salt. Add apples and nuts. Pour into greased pie plate and bake 25 to 30 minutes in 350-degree oven. Cut into wedges and serve warm or cold with whipped cream.

Mary Fry, Wichita, 1964

Pink Squirrel Pie

1 ½ cups graham cracker crumbs
⅓ cup butter, melted
½ cup cold water
1 envelope unflavored gelatin
⅓ cup sugar
⅛ teaspoon salt
3 eggs, separated
¼ cup white creme de cacao
¼ cup creme de almond
⅓ cup sugar
1 cup heavy cream
  Food coloring

Preheat oven to 350 degrees. In small bowl combine crumbs with butter. Press over bottom and sides of 9-inch pan and bake 10 minutes. Cool. Pour water into saucepan and sprinkle gelatin over it. Add ⅓ cup sugar, salt and egg yolks. Stir to blend. Place over low heat and stir until gelatin dissolves and mixture thickens. Do not boil. Remove from heat. Stir liqueurs into mixture. Chill until mixture starts to mound. Beat egg whites until stiff, then add ⅓ cup sugar and beat until peaks are firm. Fold meringue into thickened mixture. Whip the cream and add tint, if desired. Fold whipped cream into thickened mixture and turn into crust. Chill several hours or overnight. Pie freezes and thaws quite well. Makes 6 servings.

Mrs. Wayne Garrelts, Salina, 1975

Banana Ice Cream Pie

1 pint vanilla ice cream
1 cup milk
1 pkg. (4-serving size) banana instant pudding mix
1 8-inch baked pie shell or graham cracker crust

Soften ice cream in milk. Add instant pudding mix and stir until smooth. Pour filling into pie shell and allow to chill in refrigerator until set. Makes 6 to 8 servings.

Note: Variations of this recipe may be had by using different flavors of instant pudding mix.

Mrs. Paul G. Baker, Wichita, 1961

Chocolate Pecan Pie

1 cup chocolate bits
⅔ cup evaporated milk or half-and-half
2 tablespoons butter
2 eggs, beaten
1 cup sugar
2 tablespoons flour
¼ teaspoon salt
1 teaspoon vanilla
1 cup broken pecans
1 unbaked 9-inch pie shell

In small saucepan combine chocolate bits, evaporated milk and butter. Cook over low heat until mixture is creamy and smooth. In bowl combine eggs, sugar, flour, salt and vanilla. Gradually stir in chocolate mixture, then pecans. Pour into pie shell and bake in 375-degree oven 40 minutes or until firm. Makes 6 to 8 servings.

Mrs. Sam Jones, Wichita, 1975

Two-Crust Lemon Pie

Pastry for 2-crust pie
2 lemons
3 eggs
1 ½ cups sugar

Make pastry from mix or favorite recipe. Chill in refrigerator for 30 minutes, at least, then divide in half. Roll out one half and line 8-inch pie pan. Keep remainder of pastry cool until lemon filling is made. Preheat oven to 400 degrees. Grate rinds from both lemons. Peel away all white pulp and cut lemons into sections as for oranges or grapefruit. Discard seeds and connecting tissues. Work over a bowl to catch all the juice. In another bowl beat eggs slightly. Beat in sugar gradually. Combine egg mixture with lemon rind, lemon sections and all juice which has seeped out of the sections. Pour into unbaked pie shell and cover with top pastry. Seal the edges tightly. Bake in preheated oven 40 to 45 minutes or until pastry is slightly brown. Serve cool.

Mrs. Kenneth R. Roberson, Wichita, 1961

Oatmeal Pie

3 eggs, well beaten
⅔ cup white sugar
1 cup brown sugar
2 tablespoons butter
⅔ cup quick-cooking oats
⅔ cup coconut
1 teaspoon vanilla
1 unbaked 8- or 9-inch pie shell

In large bowl blend eggs, sugars, butter, oats, coconut and vanilla. Pour into unbaked pie shell. Bake at 350 degrees 30 to 35 minutes. Makes 6 to 8 servings.
Note: This tastes very much like pecan pie, but is less rich.

Mrs. Fred Heller, Elmo, 1961

Pumpkin Cheese Pie

1 pkg. (3 oz.) cream cheese
¼ cup sugar
1 egg
¼ teaspoon vanilla
1 unbaked 9-inch piecrust with high edge
2 eggs, slightly beaten
1 cup canned pumpkin
⅔ cup sugar less 2 tablespoons
1 teaspoon cinnamon
¼ teaspoon ginger
¼ teaspoon nutmeg
¼ teaspoon salt
1 cup evaporated milk
Whipped cream (for garnish, optional)

In small bowl combine softened cream cheese with ¼ cup sugar, 1 egg and ¼ teaspoon vanilla. Mix well and spread evenly in bottom of pie shell. Preheat oven to 425 degrees. In large bowl mix eggs, pumpkin, sugar, spices and salt. Mix well. Add evaporated milk and mix thoroughly. Pour over cream cheese mixture. Bake at 425 degrees for 20 minutes. Reduce heat to 350 degrees and continue baking 45 minutes. Serve with whipped cream, if desired. Makes 6 to 8 servings.

Margaret Hattan, Wichita, 1975

Frosty Lime Pie

½ cups smooth applesauce
1 pkg. (3 oz.) lime-flavored gelatin
¾ cup sugar
1 cup very cold evaporated milk
1 tablespoon lime or lemon juice
1 9-inch graham cracker or chocolate crumb crust
Thin slices of lime or kiwifruit for garnish

In medium saucepan bring applesauce to boil. Stir in gelatin and sugar. Cool completely. Whip evaporated milk and lime juice

Frosty Lime Pie — continued

in very cold bowl with very cold beaters until mixture holds stiff peaks when dropped from a spoon. Fold into gelatin mixture and pour into piecrust. Refrigerate at least 1 hour. (Can be made the day before serving.) Garnish with slices of lime or kiwifruit. Makes 8 servings.

I first used this recipe 20 years ago, when I was in high school. It's a pretty green color for the holidays, light and cool for summer.

Peg Bowman, Wichita, 1986

Sawdust Pie

1 ½ cups sugar
1 ½ cups graham cracker crumbs
1 ½ cups shredded coconut
1 ½ cups chopped pecans or walnuts, coarsely chopped
 ½ cup chocolate chips
 7 egg whites
 1 unbaked 10-inch pie shell
 Whipped cream or whipped topping

In large mixing bowl, by hand, combine sugar, crumbs, coconut, nuts, chocolate chips and egg whites (this will turn into a gooey mixture). Turn it into the pie shell. Bake in 350-degree oven for 35 to 40 minutes or until center is firm. Do not cut until cooled to just warm. Serve with whipped cream or topping. Makes 8 or more servings.

This is one of the famous desserts served at The Hungry Potter restaurant in Marshall, Texas, and is so rich it is almost sinful! I ate there while vacationing this summer, and three of us split just one piece of pie. Of course, all of us just had to get this recipe!

Patsy Elder, Wichita, 1987

MISCELLANEOUS

Grenadine Peach Cobbler

1 **cup sugar**
3 **tablespoons flour**
2 **tablespoons cornstarch**
⅛ **teaspoon nutmeg**
6 **cups sliced fresh peaches**
2 **tablespoons grenadine syrup**
1 **tablespoon lemon juice**
2 **tablespoons butter or margarine**
Pastry for 9-inch pie

In mixing bowl combine sugar, flour, cornstarch and nutmeg; mix well. Add peaches, grenadine and lemon juice; toss gently. Let stand 5 minutes. Lightly grease an 8-inch square baking dish. Add peach mixture. Dot with butter. Roll pastry on floured surface into 8-inch square. Place over peach mixture, sealing edges to the side of the dish. Cut slits in pastry. Bake at 350 degrees 55 minutes or until golden brown. Makes 6 servings.

An easy-to-make and delicious peach cobbler.

Caren Rowland, Eudora, 1990

Danish Pastry Apple Bar

5 cups all-purpose flour
2 teaspoons salt
2 cups shortening
2 eggs, separated
1 to 1⅓ cups milk
3 lbs. tart apples, pared and sliced
1 to 1 ½ cups sugar
2 teaspoons cinnamon
1 teaspoon allspice
1 ½ cups crushed cornflakes
   Margarine squares to dot filling
½ cup raisins
   Sugar
Glaze
2 cups confectioners' sugar
3 to 6 tablespoons hot water
½ teaspoon vanilla

Preheat oven to 375 degrees. Well grease a large (15½x10½x1½-inch jelly roll pan. In large bowl combine flour and salt. Cut in shortening. Beat 1 egg yolk, pour into measuring cup; add enough milk to measure ⅔ cup liquid. Repeat with second egg yolk. Mix well with flour mixture. This will be a stiff mixture; add more milk if too stiff. Place in refrigerator for 30 minutes. Meanwhile, mix apple slices with spices and sugar in large bowl. Roll out 2 crusts to fit pan. Line pan with 1 crust, sprinkle on crushed cornflakes, apples, margarine squares and raisins. Top with other crust, seal crust edges. With pastry brush, brush on beaten egg whites to cover top crust. Cut in decorated design on top, sprinkle lightly with sugar and bake 50 to 60 minutes. Meanwhile, combine confectioners' sugar, hot water and vanilla in small bowl. When pastry is done, glaze, while hot, with confectioners' sugar mixture. Cut into bars to serve. Makes 15 to 20 servings.

This is a time-consuming recipe to make, but the reward is the pleasure to those who eat it. This recipe is great for potluck dinners, picnics, family reunions or just for something special for your family.

Gwen A. Young, Wichita, 1987

Rhubarb Oatmeal Crumble

½ cup sifted all-purpose flour
¼ teaspoon salt
2 cups rolled oats (uncooked)
2 cups sugar (divided use)
½ cup butter, melted
6 cups diced fresh rhubarb
1 teaspoon cinnamon
1 tablespoon water
Ice cream (optional)

Into bowl sift together flour and salt. Add rolled oats and ¾ cup sugar. Blend butter into dry ingredients with pastry blender until mixture is crumbly. Press half of this mixture into an even layer over the bottom of a shallow casserole. Combine rhubarb, remaining 1¼ cups sugar, cinnamon and water in saucepan. Cover tightly and heat slowly just until rhubarb is hot. Pour into casserole over crumb mixture. Spread remaining oat mixture in an even layer over rhubarb. Bake in 350-degree oven until lightly browned and bubbly around edges, about 30 minutes. Serve warm, plain or with ice cream. Makes 8 servings.

Mrs. James Williams, Wichita, 1962

Ginger Snapples

3 cups raw apples, peeled, cored and sliced
1 tablespoon lemon juice
½ cup sugar
18 gingersnaps, crushed
½ cup butter

Arrange apples in a 10x6x2-inch baking dish; sprinkle with lemon juice. In small bowl combine sugar, gingersnaps and butter until crumbly. Spread over apples. Bake in 350-degree oven 30 minutes. May be eaten plain or with a favorite sauce. Makes 6 servings.

Brenda Glass, Dexter, 1965

Baked Pineapple Dressing

½ cup butter
1 cup sugar
4 eggs
1 can (8 oz.) crushed pineapple (do not drain)
⅓ cup milk
7 slices bread, cubed

In large bowl cream butter and sugar. Beat in eggs, one at a time. Stir in pineapple and milk. Fold in bread cubes and turn into a greased 8-inch square baking dish. Bake at 350 degrees for 1 hour. Makes 4 to 6 servings.

Mrs. Alred Neig, Wichita, 1969

Rhubarb Dream Dessert

1 cup all-purpose flour
5 tablespoons confectioners' sugar
½ cup margarine
2 eggs, beaten
1 ½ cups sugar
¼ cup all-purpose flour
¾ teaspoon salt
2 cups chopped rhubarb

In small bowl mix flour, confectioners' sugar and margarine with pastry blender; pat in the bottom of a 7x11-inch baking dish or pan. Bake in 350-degree oven 15 minutes. In small bowl combine eggs, sugar, flour, salt and rhubarb; pour into baked crust. Bake 35 minutes longer. Makes 6 servings.

Mrs. Ralph Boys, Logan, 1967

Tortoni Squares

⅓ to ½ cup chopped or slivered almonds
6 tablespoons melted butter
2 cups fine vanilla wafer crumbs
2 teaspoons almond extract
1 quart vanilla ice cream
1 jar (12 oz.) apricot or peach preserves
Whipped cream and maraschino cherries for garnish

In large bowl combine almonds, butter, crumbs and extract; mix well. Save ½ cup of crumb mixture for topping. Sprinkle half of the remaining crumb mixture over the bottom of a 9-inch square pan that has been lined with foil. Spoon half of ice cream over the crumb mixture; spread with half the preserves and sprinkle with remaining crumb mixture. Repeat ice cream and preserves layers. Sprinkle reserved ½ cup crumb mixture over the top. Store in freezer until ready to serve. Cut in squares and garnish with whipped cream and cherries. Makes about 9 servings.

Tortoni squares make a pretty dessert that can be taken from the freezer for any occasion.

Helen Nixon, Emporia, 1986

Lime Cheesecake

Crust
  1 cup graham cracker crumbs
  2 tablespoons sugar
  ¼ cup melted butter
Filling
  3 pkgs. (8 oz. each) cream cheese, softened
  3 eggs
  1 cup sugar
  ¼ cup lime juice
  2 tablespoons grated lime rind
Topping
  1 ½ cups sour cream
  2 tablespoons sugar
  1 tablespoon lime juice
  1 kiwifruit, sliced

Have ingredients at room temperature. Combine crumbs, sugar and butter. Press into bottom and sides of an 8-inch springform pan or bottom of a 9-inch springform pan. Bake 5 minutes in 250-degree oven. Mix 8 oz. cream cheese and 1 egg. Blend thoroughly. Add remaining cream cheese and eggs alternately, beating well after each addition. Add sugar and lime juice and beat at medium speed 10 minutes. Stir in lime rind. Pour into crust and bake 25 minutes at 350 degrees. Turn off heat and leave in oven for 45 minutes. For topping, in small bowl combine sour cream, sugar and lime juice. Spread over warm cake. Return to 350-degree oven and bake for 10 minutes. Cool on rack for several hours or overnight before removing from pan. Refrigerate. Garnish with kiwifruit just before serving. Makes 10 servings.

Mrs. Steve Fisher, Hutchinson, 1987

Neufchatel Cheesecakes

      1 pkg. (3 oz.) Neufchatel cheese
      ½ cup saltine cracker crumbs
      1 cup sugar
      4 eggs
      1 tablespoon butter, melted
      ½ cup cream or rich milk
      ½ teaspoon salt
        Grated rind of 1 lemon
        Juice of ½ lemon
      ¼ teaspoon nutmeg
      ½ cup currants
        All-purpose flour
        Rich pastry

Crumble cheese into small bowl and mix well with cracker crumbs. In another bowl beat sugar and eggs until light; add cracker and cheese mixture; mix. Add butter, cream, salt, lemon rind, lemon juice and nutmeg. Dredge currants in flour and stir into cheese mixture. Line 12 muffin cups or patty pans with rich pastry. Pour in cheese filling. Bake to 15 to 20 minutes in 425-degree oven. Makes 12 individual cakes.

Mrs. Charles Earnest, Danville, 1955

Frozen Dessert

      1 quart buttermilk
      2 cups sugar (or less)
      1 can (20 oz.) crushed pineapple, drained
      1 pkg. (16 oz.) frozen strawberries (sweetened), partially
        thawed
      5 or 6 bananas, thinly sliced

In large bowl combine buttermilk, sugar, pineapple, strawberries and bananas. Divide into foil-lined cupcake tins. Bag or package after freezing. Makes about 40. Allow to thaw slightly before serving.

Grace Smith, Mulvane, 1981

Frozen Apple Rolls

2 **cups all-purpose flour**
2 **teaspoons baking powder**
1 **teaspoon salt**
⅔ **cup shortening**
½ **cup milk**
2 ½ **cups grated raw apples**
Syrup
2 **cups sugar**
2 **cups water**
¼ **teaspoon cinnamon**
¼ **teaspoon nutmeg**
6 **to 10 drops red food coloring**
2 **tablespoons margarine**
   Cream or milk

Sift flour, baking powder and salt into large bowl. Cut in short-ening until mixture resembles coarse crumbs. Add milk all at once and stir until flour is moistened. On a lightly floured surface, roll dough into an 18x12-inch rectangle about ¼ inch thick. Spread grated raw apples on dough and roll like a jelly roll. Cut into 8 or 10 pieces. Place in plastic bags and freeze.

When ready to bake, place in an ungreased 11½x7½x1½-inch pan. Make syrup by combining sugar, water, cinnamon, nutmeg, food coloring and margarine in saucepan. Bring to boil, then pour over the frozen apple rolls. Bake at 375 degrees 35 to 40 minutes. Serve warm with cream or milk. Makes 8 to 10 servings.

Verna Shoemaker, Hesston, 1978

Phony Spumoni

1 pkg. (2 oz.) dessert topping mix
Dash of green food coloring
½ teaspoon peppermint flavoring
¼ cup quartered green and red maraschino cherries
4 tablespoons chopped candied fruit mix
1 tablespoon chopped toasted almonds
1 quart chocolate chip ice cream
Commercial spray-type whipped cream

Prepare dessert topping mix according to package directions. Fold in food coloring to make light green tint. Fold in peppermint flavoring, cherries, candied fruit and almonds; set aside. Soften ice cream. Press ice cream around sides and bottom of a 6-cup mold or bowl. Fill center of ice cream ring with dessert topping mixture. Cover and freeeze for 6 to 8 hours. To serve, unmold by pressing hot, damp towel around mold turned upside down on serving plate. Garnish with whipped cream. Makes 6 to 8 servings.

Note: If candied fruit is not available, gumdrops may be used. Also, other food coloring combinations or ice cream flavors may be substituted. Strawberry and cherry ice cream make a pretty color.

Mrs. George Medlock, Topeka, 1978

Ginger Cream

1 box (8 oz.) gingersnaps
2 cups whipping cream

In chilled bowl whip 1 cup cream until soft peaks form. Sandwich gingersnaps together with whipped cream. Wrap cream-sandwiched gingersnaps in aluminum foil. Place in refrigerator and leave overnight. Just before serving, whip 1 cup cream until soft peaks form. Spread cream over sandwiched gingersnaps, thickly. Serve immediately. Leftovers may be stored in the refrigerator or freezer (thaw before serving). Makes about 6 servings.

Emma Hanlon, Rose Hill, 1984

Jeweled Pudding

1 can (20 oz.) fruit cocktail
2 envelopes plain gelatin
⅓ cup orange juice
3 cups commercially prepared eggnog
1 ½ cups whipping cream
¼ teaspoon salt
¼ cup sugar
1 ½ teaspoons vanilla
1 tablespoon grated orange rind
1 dozen ladyfingers
Whipped cream (for garnish)

Thoroughly drain fruit cocktail; set aside. In saucepan soften gelatin in orange juice. Stir over hot water until gelatin dissolves. In another saucepan heat eggnog to lukewarm. Stir in gelatin mixture. Chill until partially set (mixture will mound on spoon). Whip whipping cream with salt, sugar and vanilla. Add orange rind and fold into eggnog mixture. Fold in 2 cups fruit cocktail. Line a 2-quart mold with ladyfingers. Spoon in pudding. Chill until set, about 4 hours. Turn out onto a plate or cake stand. Garnish with remaining fruit cocktail and whipped cream.
Makes 8 to 10 servings.

Mrs. Joseph B. Crowther, Salina, 1959

COOKIES AND CANDIES

Crushed lemon drops, peppermint sticks and cornflakes are some of the unusual ingredients in prizewinning Favorite Recipe Contest cookies and candies.

Contestants have never failed to send variations of chocolate chip, peanut butter and oatmeal cookies, the all-time favorites. Easy peanut butter cookies and unusual oatmeal cookies are made without flour.

Drop and bar cookies have been favored by contestants through the years. Bar cookies, once baked in 8-inch square or 9-by-13-inch pans, now often go into a jelly roll pan so that the cook will have a generous supply of about 40 sweets. Many bar cookies are baked in layers, and some resemble candy.

In three decades the number of candy recipes submitted has decreased, with popcorn and granola-like treats taking their place as homemade family favorites.

COOKIES

Cashew Caramel Yummies

¾ cup all-purpose flour
½ teaspoon baking powder
¼ teaspoon salt
2 eggs
½ cup sugar
¾ cup brown sugar (divided use)
½ cup and ⅓ cup chopped cashews
2 tablespoons butter or margarine
1 ½ tablespoons light cream
   Shortening

Grease 9x9-inch pan with shortening. Sift flour, baking powder and salt. In large bowl combine eggs, sugar and ½ cup brown sugar; blend on low speed 30 seconds. Stir in sifted mixture and ½ cup cashews; pour into prepared pan. Bake in 350-degree oven 20 to 25 minutes. Meanwhile, melt butter in pan over low heat. Remove from heat and stir in ¼ cup brown sugar, light cream and ⅓ cup cashews. Spread sugar mixture over baked mixture. Place 4 to 5 inches below broiling unit and broil 1 to 3 minutes until topping bubbles and is lightly browned. Cut while warm and cool in pan. Makes 16 squares.

Lori Devaney, Wichita, 1987

Mixed Nut Bars

1 ½ cups all-purpose flour
¾ cup brown sugar, packed
½ cup margarine
1 can (13 oz.) mixed nuts
½ cup light corn syrup
2 tablespoons margarine
6 oz. butterscotch pieces

Heat oven to 350 degrees. In a 9x13-inch baking pan, mix until crumbly the flour, brown sugar and ½ cup margarine. Pat mixture evenly over bottom of pan. Bake 10 minutes in preheated oven. Cool. Sprinkle with mixed nuts. In a small saucepan, over low heat, combine syrup, 2 tablespoons margarine and butterscotch pieces. Stir frequently until mixture has melted and is well blended. Pour mixture over nuts; bake in preheated oven 10 minutes. Cool before cutting. Makes about 2 dozen bars.

To cut down on the expense of the mixed nuts, I buy them when they are on sale and store them until needed.

Rosemary Sherman, Chanute, 1988

Wheat-Oat Cookies

1 ⅓ cups all-purpose flour
2 ¼ cups whole-wheat flour
1 teaspoon baking soda
1 teaspoon cinnamon
¼ teaspoon nutmeg
1 cup margarine
1 cup packed brown sugar
1 cup granulated sugar
¼ cup honey
1 cup milk
1 egg
1 teaspoon vanilla
1 cup rolled oats
1 ¾ cups raisins or chopped dates
½ cup chopped nuts

Wheat-Oat Cookies — continued

In medium bowl combine flours, soda and spices. In large bowl cream margarine and sugars; stir in honey, milk, egg and vanilla. Add dry ingredients mixture and mix well. Stir in oats, dried fruit and nuts. Drop by teaspoonfuls 2 inches apart onto greased cookie sheets. Bake 12 to 14 minutes in preheated 350-degree oven. Makes 8 to 9 dozen cookies.

This is a chewy, rich cookie with whole grains and spices.

Parma Harris, Kingman, 1990

Butter Pretzels

  ½ **lb. butter (not margarine)**
1 ⅛ **cups sugar**
  2 **eggs**
3 ¾ **cups all-purpose flour**
    Juice of 1 lemon
  1 **teaspoon vanilla**
Topping
  ½ **cup sugar**
  1 **teaspoon cinnamon**

In large bowl thoroughly mix butter and sugar. Add eggs and mix. Add flour, lemon juice and vanilla; mix well. Chill dough for several hours. Pinch off small pieces of dough, roll into ropes, then bring both ends to middle, making a pretzel shape. Bake in 375-degree oven until golden (about 10 minutes). Combine sugar and cinnamon in shallow dish. Roll cookies in cinnamon-sugar mixture. Makes 4 to 6 dozen.

My grandmother brought this recipe from Austria. It was not written down until recent years so there are several versions in my family. But it is especially enjoyed at Christmastime in our family and many of our friends have joined in the tradition.

Sheryl Songer, Hays, 1990

White Chocolate Chip and Macadamia Nut Cookies

1 ½ sticks butter (no substitute), room temperature
1 cup sugar
½ cup brown sugar
2 teaspoons vanilla
2 eggs, room temperature
2 ¼ cups all-purpose flour
1 teaspoon baking soda
1 teaspoon salt
1 cup coarsely chopped macadamia nuts
16 oz. white chocolate (or vanilla) chips

In large bowl beat butter, sugars, vanilla and eggs until light and fluffy. Mix flour with soda and salt; blend into butter mixture. Stir in nuts and chips. Chill 1 hour. Drop by rounded teaspoonfuls 2 inches apart on ungreased cookie sheets. Bake in 350-degree oven 10 to 12 minutes (until lightly browned). Cool 2 minutes before removing from pans. Makes 4 dozen.

Janie A. Noller, Wichita, 1986

Moth Cookies

2 sticks (I cup) butter
½ cup sugar
2 ½ cups all-purpose flour
¾ cup finely ground almonds

In large mixing bowl cream butter and sugar. Work in flour, a little at a time. Add almonds and knead into dough. Shape dough into 2 rolls. Chill at least 2 hours. Slice ⅛ inch thick; put on cookie sheet. Bake in 325-degree oven until light brown, 12 to 15 minutes. Makes 4 dozen.

M.J. Snyder, Wichita, 1984

Summer Coconut Bars

½ cup butter or margarine, softened
4 ½ tablespoons confectioners' sugar
1 cup all-purpose flour
Topping
3 eggs, beaten
2 tablespoons all-purpose flour
¾ cup coconut
½ teaspoon salt
1 ½ cups light brown sugar
1 teaspoon almond flavoring
¼ teaspoon baking powder
½ cup walnuts or pecans (optional)

In large bowl cream butter or margarine, sugar and all-purpose flour; work mixture into ball; roll or pat into bottom of 9x13-inch pan. Bake at 350 degrees 12 minutes. While crust mixture is baking, mix in large bowl the eggs, flour, coconut, salt, brown sugar, almond flavoring and baking powder. Chop nuts finely. Pour coconut mixture over baked crust and bake. Sprinkle chopped nuts over topping, if desired, before baking. Bake 25 minutes in preheated 350-degree oven. Makes 24 large or 32 small bars.

Barbara Livingston, Cottonwood Falls, 1984

Easy Peanut Butter Cookies

> 1 cup chunk-style peanut butter
> 1 cup sugar
> 1 egg
> 1 teaspoon vanilla

In large bowl mix peanut butter and sugar; stir in egg and vanilla (no flour). Shape into 1-inch balls and put on ungreased cookie sheets. Press with fork to flatten slightly and bake 12 to 15 minutes in 350-degree oven. Makes 3 dozen.

Note: There is NO flour in this recipe.

Mrs. D.E. McJunkin, Toronto, 1969

Unusual Oatmeal Cookies

> 4 cups quick-cooking oatmeal
> 1 cup oil
> 2 cups brown sugar
> 2 eggs, beaten
> 1 teaspoon salt
> 1 teaspoon vanilla
> 1 cup raisins (optional)
> 1 cup nuts (optional)

The night before baking cookies, combine oatmeal, oil and brown sugar in mixing bowl. In the morning, beat eggs and add to oatmeal mixture. Add salt and vanilla. Add raisins and nuts, if desired. Drop by teaspoonfuls onto greased baking sheet. Bake 12 to 15 minutes in 325-degree oven. Makes 3 to 4 dozen cookies.

Note: There is NO flour in this recipe.

Mrs. Edwin Hutchins, Wichita, 1978

Coconut Crisp Cookies

1 cup brown sugar
1 cup granulated sugar
1 cup shortening
2 eggs, beaten
1 ½ cups all-purpose flour
½ teaspoon salt
1 teaspoon soda
3 cups rolled oats
2 tablespoons shredded coconut
1 teaspoon vanilla

In large bowl cream sugars and shortening; add eggs. Sift flour with salt and soda and add to creamed mixture. Add oats, coconut and vanilla. Mixture will be very stiff. Form into small balls and press flat on cookie sheet. Bake 12 to 15 minutes in 375-degree oven. Makes 5 to 6 dozen cookies.

Mrs. D.E. Stowell, Wichita, 1956

Peppermint Sticks

2 cups all-purpose flour
1 cup sugar
1 cup butter or margarine
1 egg, separated
1 teaspoon vanilla extract
1 pkg. (6 oz.) semisweet chocolate pieces (1 cup)
½ cup crushed peppermint candy

In large mixing bowl combine flour, sugar, butter, egg yolk and vanilla extract. Blend well. Stir in chocolate pieces. Spread in ungreased 15x10-inch jelly roll pan. Beat egg white until frothy. Brush over bars. Spread crushed peppermint candy over egg white. Bake in 350-degree oven 25 to 30 minutes or until golden brown. Cool slightly. Cut into bars. Makes 40.

Patricia Hake, Wichita, 1970

Lemon Crunch Cookies

1 cup shortening
2 cups sugar
2 eggs, well beaten
1 teaspoon lemon flavoring
3 ½ cups sifted all-purpose flour
½ teaspoon salt
2 teaspoons baking powder
1 cup finely crushed lemon drops

In large bowl cream shortening and sugar. Add eggs and flavoring. Blend thoroughly. Sift together flour, salt and baking powder. Add to creamed mixture; blend thoroughly. Add crushed lemon drops in small quantities, mixing thoroughly. Form into rolls. Chill in refrigerator overnight. Slice. Bake on ungreased baking sheets in 350-degree oven 10 to 12 minutes. Makes 5 to 6 dozen.

Susan Smoll, Wichita, 1960

Cream Cheese Kipfels

2 pkgs. (8 oz. each) cream cheese
1 lb. butter or margarine
4 cups all-purpose flour
   Apricot filling (see recipe)

Allow cream cheese and butter to soften at room temperature. Beat together in large bowl. Add flour. Divide dough into 4 equal parts. Wrap individually in waxed paper; chill at least overnight.

When ready to prepare kipfels, take one portion at a time from refrigerator to work, as dough is easier to handle when chilled. Roll dough on floured and (granulated) sugared cloth to ¼- to ⅛-inch thickness. Cut with pizza wheel or knife into 3-inch squares. Fill with desired filling (1 teaspoon each). Bring two opposite corners of dough together over filling and pinch to seal. Place on ungreased cookie sheet. Bake in 400-degree oven 12 to 15 minutes. Makes approximately 7 to 8 dozen.

Apricot filling: Cook 1 lb. dried apricots as package directs, except lengthen cooking time to 30 minutes. Sweeten to taste. Beat with mixer or place in food processor until pureed. A commercial filling may also be used.

Mrs. A.W. Badman, Wichita, 1969

Millionaire Nuggets

½ cup butter
2 cups light brown sugar
½ teaspoon salt
3 eggs, beaten
2 ½ cups all-purpose flour
1 teaspoon soda
2 tablespoons hot water
1 lb. pecans, chopped
1 lb. candied cherries, chopped
3 tablespoons brandy or wine
2 teaspoons vanilla

In large bowl cream butter, brown sugar and salt. Add beaten eggs, flour, soda which has been dissolved in hot water, nuts, cherries, brandy or wine and vanilla. Spoon into gem-size paper baking cups in mini-muffin tins. Bake 10 minutes in 350-degree oven. Makes about 5 dozen.

Note: These can be made weeks ahead of the holiday season and frozen.

Mrs. Robert Hooper, McPherson, 1969

CANDIES

Hi-Energy Trail Bars

1 cup sugar
1 cup honey
1 cup peanut butter
1 cup wheat germ
1 cup rolled oats
5 cups dry cereal (high protein, rice or oats)

In large pot boil sugar and honey 1 minute. Add peanut butter and mix. Add dry cereals. Mix and press into 9x13-inch pan. Cut into 1 1/2-inch squares. Makes 40.

Note: Additional optional ingredients may be nuts, coconut, baking chips, raisins, sunflower seeds, etc. These bars keep well without refrigeration, or can be kept under refrigeration successfully for eight or nine months.

Bobbie Harms, Wichita, 1977

Honey Candy

1 cup honey
¾ cup non-fat dry milk (unreconstituted)
1 cup rolled oats
½ cup peanut butter
½ cup chopped peanuts or other nuts
½ cup chocolate chips
½ cup raisins

In large saucepan boil honey 4 minutes, stirring to keep from burning. Add dry milk, oats, peanut butter, peanuts, chocolate chips and raisins. Pour into buttered 9x9-inch pan. Cut into squares when cool. Wrap in waxed paper. Makes about 3 dozen small pieces.

Ruby Koehn, Dodge City, 1986

Almond Barkies

2 cups crispy rice cereal
2 cups crunchy peanut butter cereal
2 cups dry-roasted peanuts
2 cups miniature marshmallows
1 ½ lbs. almond bark
Colored sugar (optional)

Measure cereals, peanuts and marshmallows into large mixing bowl. Grate almond bark and melt in top of double boiler, stirring constantly. Pour melted bark slowly over ingredients in mixing bowl, mixing while pouring. Drop by teaspoons onto waxed paper and allow to dry. Sprinkle with colored sugar if desired. Store in airtight container. Makes 75 to 80 almond barkies.

I found this recipe eight years ago in an insurance magazine! They are standard around our house at Christmas. Our three boys love to help make them.

Kathy Garriott, Wichita, 1990

Mom's Creamy Oat Fudge

1 cup sugar
1 cup marshmallow creme
⅓ cup evaporated milk
¼ cup margarine
¼ teaspoon salt
1 cup semisweet chocolate chips
1 teaspoon vanilla
¾ cup quick-cooking oats
½ cup chopped nuts

Combine sugar, marshmallow creme, evaporated milk, margarine and salt in 2-quart saucepan. Cook over low heat, stirring constantly until mixture boils. Remove from heat and add semisweet chocolate chips. Stir until chips are completely melted. Stir in vanilla, quick oats and nuts. Pour into buttered 8-inch pan. Refrigerate. Makes 2 dozen pieces.

I got this recipe from my mother several years ago. It has always been one of my favorites as it is easy to make and does not use as much sugar as most fudge recipes. Last Christmas I made 11 batches for my boyfriend to take to work. Needless to say, he married me in March!

Stephanie Schroeder, Wichita, 1989

Four Nut Brittle

¾ cup broken pecans
¾ cup broken walnuts
¾ cup broken almonds
¾ cup broken filberts
1 ½ cups sugar
1 cup light corn syrup
½ cup butter
1 teaspoon vanilla
1 teaspoon orange extract

In jelly roll pan toast nuts in 325-degree oven 15 minutes, stirring twice. Butter a heavy 3-quart saucepan. In saucepan combine sugar, corn syrup and butter. Cook over medium heat to boiling, stirring constantly with wooden spoon. Using a candy thermometer, cook over medium heat, without stirring. When mixture reaches 290 degrees (soft crack stage), remove from heat. Stir in vanilla and orange extract. Stir in warm nuts. Turn candy mixture out onto buttered baking sheet; spread evenly. Cool. Break brittle into pieces. Makes 2¼ lbs.

This candy is a holiday favorite at our house.

Anne Catherine Pierce, Winfield, 1987

Holiday Wreath

30 marshmallows
½ cup butter
1 teaspoon vanilla
2 teaspoons green food coloring
3 ½ cups cornflakes
Red candied cherries
Silver dragees

Heat marshmallows, butter, vanilla and food coloring over very low heat or in top of double boiler until marshmallows and butter are melted, stirring frequently. Gradually add cornflakes until well coated. Drop on waxed paper. Shape into wreath with oiled hands or wooden spoon. Decorate with cherries and dragees. Makes one 9-inch wreath. A candle may be used in the center. To serve, cut into wedges.

Note: This confection may be tinted any color or shaped in any fashion for holidays around the calendar. For instance, shape into a heart and decorate with tiny heart-shaped candies for Valentine's Day, or add no coloring and decorate with pecan halves or candy corn for a Thanksgiving wreath.

Mrs. Walter Franklin, Salina, 1973

Pecan Nut Caramels

¾ cup finely chopped pecans
2 cups sugar
½ cup butter or margarine
¾ cup light corn syrup
2 cups evaporated milk

Butter an 8x8x2-inch pan and sprinkle evenly with half of pecans. Combine sugar, butter and corn syrup in medium saucepan. Stir in 1 cup evaporated milk. Bring to boil over medium heat, stirring constantly. Add remaining evaporated milk slowly so that mixture continues to boil. Cook, stirring constantly, over medium heat until candy forms a firm ball in cold water. Pour hot caramel over pecans in prepared pan. Sprinkle top with remaining pecans. Cool and cut into squares; separate to dry.

Alice Penland, Wichita, 1975

Lemon Coconut Kisses

3 egg whites, at room temperature
1 teaspoon salt
3 cups sifted confectioners' sugar
2 cups shredded coconut
½ teaspoon lemon extract
  Few drops of yellow food coloring
  Confectioners' sugar
2 oz. semisweet chocolate or chocolate chips (optional)

Beat egg whites and salt slightly. Gradually add confectioners' sugar. Beat smooth after each addition. Add coconut and extract, mixing well. Add food coloring to tint a delicate, light yellow. Mix well. Cover a cookie sheet with waxed paper, then sprinkle with confectioners' sugar. Shape candy with a teaspoon into peaks, then place on waxed paper. Let stand 30 to 40 minutes. Melt chocolate over hot, not boiling, water. With a teaspoon, drizzle a small amount of chocolate on top of each peak. Let stand until set. Makes about 30 kisses.

Mrs. Gerald Wilhite, Emporia, 1976

Honey Chocolate Fudge

- **2 squares chocolate**
- **2 cups sugar**
- **⅛ teaspoon salt**
- **⅔ cup sweetened condensed milk**
- **¼ cup honey**
- **1 teaspoon vanilla**
- **2 tablespoons butter**
- **⅓ cup chopped pecans**

Chop chocolate into large saucepan and combine with sugar, salt, sweetened condensed milk and honey. Cook over moderate heat, stirring often enough to avoid burning. Cook until candy thermometer temperature shows 236 degrees or soft ball stage. Remove from heat and add vanilla and butter. Allow to cool to 110 degrees or until pan is no longer hot to the touch. Beat until it begins to firm and fold in nuts. Pour into buttered 8x8-inch pan. Cut when firm.

Mrs. Glasco W. Rector, Wichita, 1958

Easter Egg Candy

¼ **lb. butter**
2 **lbs. confectioners' sugar**
1 **teaspoon vanilla**
¼ **cup evaporated milk**
2 **cups grated fresh coconut**
2 **cups finely ground almonds**
¼ **cup maraschino cherries**
¼ **cup chopped walnuts**
  Dipping chocolate

In large bowl cream butter and add confectioners' sugar, vanilla, milk, coconut and almonds. Beat with electric mixer until very light, then add maraschino cherries and walnuts. Cover with waxed paper and let ripen at least 1 week in refrigerator. Shape into eggs and place on waxed paper. Ripen until surface becomes crusty. Turn over so underside moisture is evaporated. Place dipping chocolate in small pan over boiling water. When chocolate is melted and lukewarm, beat well with a spoon. Using two forks, gently lift an egg into the dip and out. Place the covered egg on a lightly buttered flat dish or pan. Cool and allow chocolate to dry.

Mrs. Everett McJunkin, Toronto, 1958

Mexican Orange Candy

3 cups sugar (divided use)
1 ½ cups hot milk
Grated rind of 2 oranges
½ cup butter or margarine
1 cup chopped pecans

Melt 1 cup sugar in heavy 2-quart pan. When sugar is melted to rich golden color, add milk heated almost to boiling. Add milk gradually, stirring quickly. Add remaining 2 cups sugar, stirring until dissolved. Cook until candy forms an almost hard ball (238 degrees on candy thermometer). Remove pan from heat and add grated orange rind, butter and nuts. Beat until candy is creamy but still soft enough to pour into 9-inch square buttered pan. When cool, cut into 1-inch squares.

Marilyn Marshall, Hays, 1982

REQUESTED RECIPES

It's not always easy to locate the recipes that readers request, but The Eagle staff does its best.

The same recipe may be known by several names. Often when a reader recollects that a recipe was printed in The Eagle "last year," we find that it appeared two or three years previously.

The Readers Exchange column in the weekly food section enlists the aid of readers to help others find "lost" recipes. Usually several recipe collectors respond, even when the clues are vague, and we thank them for that.

Requests for recipes peak during the holiday season, and reach another high during garden harvest time when folks want recipes for using an abundance of green tomatoes and other produce.

In this chapter are some of the recipes for which we get repeated requests.

This fruitcake recipe has been requested many times since it was a Sunday Fare recipe in 1988.

Wall-to-Wall Nuts and Fruit Cake

2 sticks (1 cup) margarine
1 cup sugar
5 eggs
1 teaspoon vanilla
1 teaspoon almond flavoring
2 cups all-purpose flour
½ teaspoon baking powder
1 lb. candied pineapple (red or green)
1 lb. candied cherries
1 lb. golden raisins
1 lb. walnuts
1 lb. pecans
Cherries and pecans for decorating

Thoroughly grease a bundt or angel food cake pan. In large mixer bowl cream margarine and sugar. Beat in eggs, vanilla and almond. In another bowl combine flour and baking powder. Chop fruits and nuts coarsely. Mix well with flour. With heavy spoon stir flour-fruit mixture into creamed mixture, blending well. Pack into prepared pan. Bake 1½ hours in 300-degree oven. Decorate with cherries and pecans as desired. Wrap airtight for storage.

For many years this was a secret recipe of the Wichita Home Economists in Business. The organization raised scholarship funds by selling the cakes during the holiday season. The recipe "went public" in the mid-1980s.

White Fruitcake

1 lb. pecans
1 lb. coconut
1 lb. mixed candied fruit
½ lb. candied cherries (whole)
1 lb. light raisins
1 can (16 oz.) sliced pineapple or pineapple tidbits, drained
½ cup flour
1 cup butter
1 cup sugar
8 eggs
3 cups flour
½ cup pineapple juice (reserved from draining pineapple)
Dash salt (optional)
1 teaspoon vanilla
Pecan halves and candied cherries for garnish

Prepare 6 small loaf pans by greasing and lining with waxed paper. In extra-large bowl combine pecans, coconut, mixed fruit, candied cherries and raisins. Cut pineapple rings into tidbits and add to mixture; toss to mix. Add ½ cup flour and toss to coat fruit with flour. In mixing bowl cream butter and sugar. Add eggs 1 at a time, beating well after each addition. Add flour alternately with pineapple juice, beating well; beat in salt and vanilla. Pour batter over mixed fruits and stir to mix. Divide batter evenly among loaf pans. Pack lightly into pans, smooth tops and decorate as desired with nuts and candied fruit. Bake in 275-degree oven for 1½ hours. Cakes should be golden on top and lightly browned around edges. Cool on racks, but remove from pans while still warm. Remove waxed paper when cakes are completely cooled. Wrap airtight in plastic wrap and aluminum foil for storage. Store in refrigerator or freezer. Makes about 6 lbs. of fruitcake.

Note: For larger pans or molds, extend baking time; for small-

White Fruitcake — continued

er cakes reduce baking time. When baking cakes in disposable aluminum foil pans, use two pans, one inside the other, to ensure even baking. Cakes may be wrapped in cheesecloth soaked with brandy or rum for aging in the refrigerator.

After fruitcake and other holiday recipes, the method for preparing Angelo's pickled eggplant is The Eagle's most requested recipe.

Angelo's Pickled Eggplant

Here's how Wichita restaurateur Angelo Fasciano "talked" Wichita Eagle home economist Kathleen Kelly through the Angelo's Restaurant recipe for pickled eggplant in September 1979:

"So much depends on the eggplant," said Fasciano. "It's best to have really fresh, tight (firm) eggplant. They're easier to peel and aren't so spongy as old eggplant."

Fasciano recommended that the home cook start with at least a bushel of eggplant to make the project worthwhile. You'll only end up with a couple of gallons of the pickle by the time you've finished the process. First, wash the eggplant and cut off the stems. Be sure to take off enough so that you have no hard core remaining. Peel the eggplant; a good vegetable peeler does the best job, though you may use a knife.

Slice the eggplant ¼ inch thick; then slice again into julienne strips. Sprinkle the strips heavily with salt (pickling or non-iodized), mixing salt and eggplant thoroughly. Place in a relatively narrow container — crockery, plastic or enameled, not aluminum. Place a plate that fits inside the container on top of the eggplant and top it with a weight. At Angelo's, a gallon container filled with water is used.

The salt and weight will remove liquid (it will be dark in color) from the eggplant. Drain this liquid and continue to squeeze the eggplant until no more liquid can be extracted. At home you can use non-aluminum steel containers, one small enough to fit inside the other, and allow the juice to overflow the smaller container into the larger, and just keep squeezing, Fasciano said.

When enough liquid has been squeezed from the eggplant, it will be a greenish-gray wad. The importance of getting all the juice out can't be overemphasized, Fasciano said. If juice is left

Angelo's Pickled Eggplant — continued

in the eggplant, it will dilute the vinegar and oil used for pickling. The juice may make the pickle bitter and reduce its keeping qualities.

Break up the mass of eggplant and place in a non-aluminum container. Bring enough white vinegar to cover — or use half vinegar and half water — to a boil and pour hot over the eggplant. Let stand 15 minutes or so to allow the vinegar to penetrate the shards of eggplant. It can be allowed to stand for several hours in the vinegar, if necessary.

Drain the vinegar from the eggplant and squeeze again, though not so dry as before; some of the vinegar flavor should be retained. Spicing has to be to your own taste, Fasciano said.

You'll need to season with salt, pepper, oregano and garlic powder or granules (not garlic salt). One Italian cookbook recommends ½ tablespoon garlic powder and 1½ tablespoons oregano for 5 pounds of whole eggplant.

Mix in spices and enough good-quality olive oil to saturate the shards of eggplant. Stir occasionally to mix well. You should be able to taste the vinegar; if not, add more to the mixture. Neither the garlic nor the oregano should dominate the flavor.

If you make a mistake and add too much of anything, correct by slicing, salting and squeezing, steeping in vinegar and squeezing another eggplant to add to the mixture.

Before storing in the refrigerator, pour a layer of oil over the top of the mixture to form a "seal" that will keep air from getting into the eggplant. Cover with a lid. Pickled eggplant should last at least a year in the refrigerator. It is a delightful addition to any antipasto or relish tray, can be tossed into a salad and even makes a piquant sandwich accent.

The recipe for 7-pound Christmas fudge was designed to be mixed in a Kitchen Aid heavy-duty mixer. It was a 1982 Sunday Fare recipe.

7-Pound Christmas Fudge

3 **large bars (8 oz. each) milk chocolate, broken in small pieces**
2 **pkgs. (11 ½ oz. each) milk chocolate bits**
1 **large jar (13 oz.) marshmallow creme**
4 **cups sugar**
1 **tall can (13 oz.) evaporated milk**
½ **lb. butter**
2 **teaspoons vanilla**
1 **cup chopped black walnuts, walnuts or pecans**

In large mixing bowl of heavy-duty electric mixer, combine broken chocolate bars, chocolate bits and marshmallow creme; set aside. In large, heavy saucepan combine sugar, evaporated milk and butter. Cook and stir over medium heat until mixture boils; boil 5 minutes. Pour hot mixture over chocolate mixture. Beat until ingredients are thoroughly blended. Beat in vanilla; remove beater and stir in chopped nuts. Quickly pour mixture into buttered 9x13-inch pan. Cool. Cover tightly and refrigerate until firm enough to cut into small squares. Flavor will be best after 1 or 2 weeks of storage. Makes about 7 lbs. fudge.

Note: Sugar may be reduced to 3 cups; there will be a little less fudge and it will be less sweet.

The flavor of this cheese blend is best with fall fruits like apples and pears, but it may be served year-round.

Three-Cheese Ring With Fruit

1 lb. cheddar cheese, grated
½ lb. Monterey Jack cheese, grated
4 oz. blue cheese, crumbled
½ cup mayonnaise
¼ cup sherry
¼ teaspoon curry powder
½ teaspoon grated lemon rind
 Fruits in season, cut in bite-size pieces
 Crackers

In large mixing bowl combine grated cheddar and Monterey Jack cheeses with blue cheese and mayonnaise; beat until thoroughly blended. Beat in sherry, curry and lemon rind. Pack into buttered 1-quart ring mold. Chill, covered, in refrigerator several hours or overnight to firm mixture and blend flavors (may be prepared several days in advance of serving). To unmold, dip mold to top in hot water, then turn cheese out onto serving plate; return to refrigerator briefly to firm surface of mold. Flavor will be richest if mold is allowed to come to room temperature before serving. Fill center and surround mold with bite-size pieces of fruit in season; serve crackers alongside. Makes about 24 servings.

Note: If desired, pack cheese mixture into several small crocks and serve in crock or unmolded. Tightly covered, cheese mixture may be refrigerated for about 30 days.

A cheese ring filled with pecans and strawberry preserves was a popular contribution to salad suppers in the late 1970s.

Cheese Ring With Strawberry Preserves

1 pkg. (16 oz.) extra-sharp cheddar cheese, shredded
1 pkg. (16 oz.) medium cheddar cheese, shredded
1 small onion, grated
1 cup real mayonnaise
1 teaspoon red pepper flakes
1 cup chopped pecans, divided
1 jar (18 oz.) strawberry preserves
Parsley for garnish
Crackers

In large bowl combine cheddar cheeses, onion, mayonnaise and red pepper. Oil or spray with non-stick coating a 7-cup ring mold or bundt pan. Sprinkle ¼ cup chopped pecans in ring; press cheese mixture into mold. Chill until firm. Dip ring in hot water and unmold on serving platter. Return to refrigerator briefly to let surface of cheese firm. Put ¾ cup chopped pecans in center of ring; top with strawberry preserves. Garnish with parsley and serve with crackers. Makes 12 to 20 servings.

Lasagna without tomato sauce and without meat is popular around the clock — from brunch to a late-night supper.

Spinach Lasagna

1 **carton (24 oz.) cottage cheese**
3 **eggs, beaten**
2 **tablespoons fresh parsley, chopped, or 1 tablespoon dried parsley (optional)**
½ **teaspoon garlic powder or 1 tablespoon minced garlic chives**
¼ **teaspoon salt**
¼ **teaspoon white pepper**
1 **pkg. (8 oz.) lasagna noodles, cooked according to package directions**
3 **pkgs. (10 oz. each) frozen spinach, thawed and squeezed dry**
8 **oz. shredded mozzarella or Monterey Jack cheese**
1 **cup grated Parmesan cheese**

In large mixing bowl combine cottage cheese, beaten eggs, parsley, garlic powder or garlic chives, salt and pepper.

Lightly grease or spray 9x13-inch baking dish. Cover bottom with layer of lasagna noodles, then a third each of the cottage cheese mixture and mozzarella or Jack cheese. Dot a third of the spinach over the cheese; top with a third of the Parmesan cheese. Repeat layers, ending with Parmesan cheese. Cover lightly with aluminum foil and bake in 350-degree oven 30 minutes. Uncover and bake an additional 15 to 20 minutes, or until lightly browned and bubbling.

Let casserole stand about 10 minutes before cutting and serving. Makes 6 to 9 servings.

Many people have requested this recipe since it was contributed to the Sunday Fare column in 1989. It has the look and flavor of bread-and-butter pickles.

Excellent Microwave Pickles

½ teaspoon salt
¼ teaspoon turmeric
¼ teaspoon mustard seed
¼ teaspoon celery seed
½ cup vinegar
1 cup sugar
2 cucumbers, unpeeled, thinly sliced
1 or 2 onions, thinly sliced

In small bowl or measuring pitcher combine salt, turmeric, mustard seed, celery seed, vinegar and sugar. Mix cucumbers and onions in large microwave-safe bowl. Pour vinegar mixture over cucumbers and onions. Microwave, uncovered, on high 5 minutes. Stir well; return to microwave 5 minutes more. Cool, pour into quart jar and refrigerate. Pickles are ready to eat when thoroughly chilled. Store in refrigerator. Makes 1 quart.

Honey jelly is a no-drip spread for toast, muffins, biscuits, etc. The addition of lemon juice and pectin makes it a little less sweet than honey. It was a 1985 Sunday Fare contribution.

Honey Jelly

3 cups honey
¾ cup water
3 tablespoons fresh lemon juice
1 pouch (3 oz.) liquid pectin

Wash half-pint canning jars, bands and lids. In large saucepan stir together honey, water and lemon juice. Bring to boil; stir in pectin. Start timing when mixture begins to boil hard; boil 1 minute. Remove from heat. With metal spoon skim off foam. Pour into clean, hot jars. Wipe rims clean and cover with hot lids. Cool on rack. Makes 4 cups. Store in refrigerator.

Meringue cookies have become popular in recent years because they are relatively low in calories, require few ingredients and are simple to put together.

Forgotten Cookies

2 egg whites at room temperature
⅔ cup sugar
   Pinch salt
1 teaspoon vanilla
1 cup chopped pecans or walnuts or mini-chips of desired flavor

Preheat oven to 350 degrees. In large bowl beat egg whites until foamy. Gradually add sugar and continue to beat until stiff. Add salt and vanilla and mix well. Add nuts or chips to mixture. Line baking sheets with aluminum foil or baking parchment; do not grease. Drop meringue mixture from teaspoon onto lined baking sheets. Place in 350-degree oven and immediately turn to off. Leave cookies in turned-off oven overnight, or at least 5 hours. Makes 2 to 3 dozen cookies.

Hot gazpacho is low-fat, low-calorie tomato-vegetable soup to which cooks have added their own touches since it first appeared in The Eagle.

Hot Gazpacho

1 can (46 oz.) tomato juice
2 tablespoons olive oil (optional)
¾ to 1 cup red wine vinegar
½ teaspoon salt
1 teaspoon paprika
¼ teaspoon garlic powder
Pinch sugar
2 tablespoons chopped cilantro or 1 teaspoon dried leaf oregano
1 can (4 oz.) chopped green chilies
2 to 4 drops hot pepper sauce
4 to 6 green onions, sliced
½ medium cucumber, diced
½ cup diced green pepper
½ cup sliced ripe olives
Lemon cartwheels for garnish

In soup kettle or slow cooker combine tomato juice, olive oil, vinegar, salt, paprika, garlic powder, sugar, cilantro or oregano, green chilies and hot pepper sauce. Bring to simmering temperature and simmer for at least 30 minutes to blend flavors. Taste and adjust seasonings as desired. Just before serving add onion, cucumber, green pepper and olives. Simmer to warm vegetables but do not cook them. Serve garnished with lemon cartwheels, if desired. Makes about 6 servings.

Note: Canned tomatoes, chopped, with juice may be substituted for part of the tomato juice. Dry red wine may be substituted for the red wine vinegar. Canned oysters (3¾ oz.) may be added with the vegetables. Or add, with vegetables, 1 can (16 oz.) garbanzo beans, drained, or about 1½ cups cooked soybeans.

When the first frost threatens, at least one caller is certain to ask for the recipe for green tomato pie. Its flavor is much like that of a green apple pie.

Green Tomato Pie

Pastry for 9-inch, 2-crust pie
1 **cup sugar**
⅓ **cup flour**
¼ **teaspoon salt**
¼ **teaspoon ground cloves**
½ **teaspoon cinnamon**
⅛ **teaspoon nutmeg**
6 **large green tomatoes, sliced ¼ inch thick (do not use stem end)**
½ **cup golden raisins**
2 **tablespoons cider vinegar**
3 **tablespoons butter**

Roll out half the dough and fit into 9-inch pie pan. Combine sugar, flour, salt, cloves, cinnamon and nutmeg in shallow bowl. Stir with fork to mix. Coat ⅓ of tomato slices at a time with sugar mixture. Spread all of the slices evenly over dough in pan. Sprinkle with raisins and top with any remaining sugar mixture. Drizzle with vinegar and dot with butter. Roll out remaining dough and cover filling with pastry. Crimp edges and cut 2 or 3 small vents in top crust. Bake in 425-degree oven 40 minutes, or until crust is golden and juices bubble around edges of pie. Serve at room temperature.

There are many versions of this recipe. It's often called end-of-garden relish.

Green Tomato Relish

1 **peck (16-18 lbs.) green tomatoes, ground**
1 **cup pickling salt**
1 **medium head cabbage, ground**
6 **sweet red peppers, ground**
6 **green peppers, ground**
6 **medium onions, ground**
8 **cups sugar**
3 **quarts vinegar**
2 **tablespoons mustard seed**
2 **tablespoons celery seed**
1 **whole clove**

In mixing bowl combine ground green tomatoes and 1 cup salt. Place in muslin bag and let drain (in non-aluminum colander suspended over a bowl) overnight.

In large, non-aluminum pot combine cabbage, red and green peppers, onion, drained green tomatoes, sugar and vinegar. Place mustard seed, celery seed and clove in tea ball or cheese-cloth bag. Cook relish, stirring occasionally, until onions are tender, about 35 minutes. Remove spices. Place relish in clean jars and seal according to manufacturer's directions. Process pints in boiling water bath 15 minutes. Makes about 20 pints.

INDEX